gardens in the sky

gardens
in the sky

inspirational ideas and planting designs
for **roof terraces** and **balconies**

Michèle Osborne

Photographs by Steven Wooster

aqua marine

Contents

introduction

The idea of creating a "garden in the sky" — a green space high up above the noise and pollution of the city — is not just a fantasy dreamt up by urbanites longing for a rural idyll, but an exhilarating reality. Although roof gardens seem to be enjoying a greater vogue than ever, they are not a new phenomenon: lavish terraces have existed since the fabled Hanging Gardens of Babylon. The challenge now is to make such gardens part of our lives in the 21st century.

left This is a perfect example of the relaxing life high in the sky on a hot summer's day, with a lunch table tantalizingly set among masses of fragrant lavender and flowering annuals in pots.

A roof garden is a privileged and wonderful space. High above life on the streets, it offers a thrilling proximity to nature, as well as privacy, outstanding views, the perfect venue for entertaining and relaxing, and somewhere to indulge in some sky-high gardening.

The mere mention of roof gardens evokes warm climates, blue skies and blazing sunsets. Even though we will probably never know exactly what the Hanging Gardens of Babylon looked like, they still fascinate us. We visualize a profusion of cascading plants fed by a shimmering network of irrigation channels. They fire our imagination because they represent an oasis, the fruit of vision, skill and affluence.

The evolution of the roof garden

In hot countries where rain is rare, a flat roof is usually an integral part of the living space and becomes the centre of life in the cool of the evening, with cooking, eating and even sleeping under the stars. Here, balconies, often hidden behind wooden screens, also provide a refuge from the heat and the outside world. In these climatic conditions, such use of space is logical and sometimes necessary, but how do we explain why roofs have become so popular in northern cities, where the weather is conducive to outdoor life for only a short season?

Over the decades, new methods and styles of building and new ways of living have seen the popularity of terraces and balconies increase. Although balconies were originally decorative architectural features with no real practical function, new construction techniques meant that they could be cantilevered, so increasing the floor area and allowing builders to offer more usable space.

The proliferation of skyscrapers in many cities across the world brought more possibilities. Penthouses appeared on top of these skyscrapers, housing utilities such as the laundry room and staff quarters. The advent of air-conditioning transformed the role of these one-storey structures, which were converted into luxury apartments with "wrap-around" terraces ready to be transformed into wonderful gardens with staggering views.

In Europe, the first significant terraces meant for living were designed back in the late 1940s by the Swiss architect Le Corbusier for La Cité Radieuse in Marseilles, a tall, slab-like building on stilts. Apartments built on two floors could expand outside on to balconies painted in primary colours. Residents were encouraged to meet on the communal roof space, which housed a crèche and a swimming pool, or on the landings in drying areas.

Another famous pioneering roof garden is that of Derry and Toms in London. Built in the late 1930s, it remains the perfect example of a fantasy garden built 30m (100ft) above the ground, complete with over 500 trees, Moorish fountains, Tudor gardens and pink flamingos.

Today, gardens in the sky can be found all over the world, and the different designs that are chosen – from bucolic country garden to minimalist, and from stark Mediterranean to Zen-like Japanese – make each one an invaluable sanctuary from the world below.

opposite This New York skyline is a startling demonstration of how roof gardens seem to spring up everywhere, adding decorative touches of green to a spectacular forest of stone, brick and concrete.

below Life is really happening on these Italian roof terraces sprawling over several houses, utilizing every inch of space for all sorts of pots and even a pergola for shade.

closer to the sky

With an ever-increasing number of people flocking to major cities over the years, and the fast-rising price of urban real estate, developers have concentrated on building upwards. As it becomes more difficult to own a garden on the ground, the potential of roof gardens as a sanctuary above the city has become apparent.

The thrill of being high up is hard to surpass. The first thing you notice as you set foot on a roof terrace is that the air seems purer. Even though you might be only a few floors above the bustle and traffic of the city, you experience an instant feeling of freedom. The sky envelops you in all its drama and vastness, evoking echoes of the feelings you might experience on top of a mountain.

The movement and shapes of clouds are mesmerizing and constantly changing, from big billowing cushions to the thinnest strands. You learn to recognize which clouds herald the approach of a downpour and which milky white expanses will gradually be blown away to reveal blue skies. Of course, none of this is new to people who live in the country or by the sea, but to town dwellers who take the time to look, it is pure magic.

Another thing you are rarely aware of at ground level is that the sun rises and sets in a different place throughout the seasons, following a huge arc in the east and west. The delicate light of dawn is almost secret in its golden glow, while the incredible layers of colours blazing through the sky at sunset, from fuchsia pink to the deepest purple, are pure theatre.

Thunderstorms take on a whole new dimension, as they can be observed in all their terrifying glory. Even rain and wind offer enjoyable experiences. Every change of weather brings a new backdrop to the city for you to contemplate. These few moments of meditative stillness, removed from the bustle of life, become priceless.

Then, at night, another wonderful display awaits you when all the familiar landmarks either disappear or are outlined by thousands of lights. Streets are sparkling ribbons, the stacked-up lights of a tall building help you to identify an area, while reflections in a river add elements of mystery to the composition. Everything appears quiet and yet strangely alive at the same time. Marvelling at this city-life light show while sharing a meal under a starlit sky is a rare pleasure that can almost make you feel you are on a summer holiday.

Roof gardens and balconies are undoubtedly privileged spaces, whether they are in London, New York or Auckland, so it is hardly surprising that they have become so highly desirable and are the setting for many remarkable designs.

below As the evening advances towards twilight, the sky is transformed with an array of vivid purples and burnt oranges stretching across the cityscape, enhanced here by the reflections in the River Thames in London.

above The landscape has been spectacularly "borrowed" here on this small London terrace by a very clever reflection, totally altering the scale and bringing a very unexpected ornament.

right Because of the views it commands, a roof terrace need be no more than an observation look-out with the minimum of furniture, but an essential telescope.

below The appeal of a roof terrace could not be more obvious than here in this lounging corner, with beautifully designed furniture surrounded by lush planting – a much-welcomed counterpoint to the hectic city beyond.

privilege and privacy

In addition to their wonderful proximity to the sky, roof terraces have many other unrivalled assets that make them privileged spaces in which to spend one's time.

The main asset, of course, is the view, whether it spreads panoramically over a country landscape or the whole of a city, or focuses on just part of an urban landscape above a tangle of roofs. The vantage point of a roof offers a surprising and otherwise unknown vision of a place that might seem quite ordinary at ground level. From your bird's eye position, you can contemplate the beauty of nature in a rural landscape or see the way in which a city has been planned, with its network of roads and tree-lined streets, a long empty corridor indicating a river, some landmarks, the stacked-up lights of tall buildings or the sunset reflected in the windows of a skyscraper – all of this diversity and richness is spread out before you to be enjoyed.

A second benefit of a roof garden is the privacy it affords. Unlike urban gardens on the ground, which are generally surrounded on all sides by other buildings, with overlooking windows and neighbouring gardens encroaching on your privacy, roof terraces feel much more like secluded havens, even if other buildings can be seen in the distance. Being high up and under the sky seems to cancel out any impression of proximity, making it possible to forget the bustle of the city while admiring it from afar. The seclusion

of the terrace's position also gives the owner more of a free hand when planning the design. With no architectural surroundings, and no nearby gardens to give a predominant style, there is a freedom to opt for whatever style is desired, whether it be lush country-garden or stark modern, with no fear of it looking out of place.

A third asset of the privileged position of the roof terrace is the amount of sunlight it receives. With few, if any, surrounding buildings to create shade, the exposure to sunlight is more intense, and with careful planning this can be used to maximum advantage for growing colourful annuals and perennials in summer, which will enhance the protective framework of mainly evergreen planting. The intense level of sunlight does, of course, bring problems too – notably a need for regular watering – but these are vastly outweighed by the benefits of a lush roof garden.

With its extraordinary combination of assets, a roof terrace is a very special and secluded place in which to relax, entertain, grow plants, and simply enjoy life in the sky.

above The planting of this city terrace brings in the trees and the landscape beyond, while the silver-grey tones of the decking, planters and furniture appear to reflect the sky.

below A lot of services end on the roof, and whereas most have to be hidden or disguised, this fantastic cluster of chimney pots, with their shiny metal cowls, do not need any camouflage.

achieving your dream

Divided into five chapters, this book deals with creating roof gardens in private residential spaces. Gardens built on top of car parks, hotels or office blocks, though often at the vanguard of design and a great source of inspiration, have very specific requirements justifying a separate book.

Chapter 1 focuses on the inner view – the terrace itself, rather than the stunning views to be seen from it – considering different ways to create an inviting space. Just as with a garden on the ground, the design vocabulary can be traditional or modern, formal or informal. But every decision will have to make the best of the very special nature of the space, with its mixture of hostile elements and unique assets, whether the terrace is used for entertaining, relaxation or private contemplation.

Once an overall design decision has been made, professionals should be involved in the construction of a garden on a roof, since this requires precise surveys and calculations. The construction also relies on immaculate hard landscaping, which, in the confines of a terrace, will be highly visible. Then comes the exciting moment of choosing the right materials to give the space its identity and establish its structure. Chapter 2 examines the many possibilities for materials for boundaries, floors and permanent structures, including toughened glass, metal, timber, natural stone, trellis and fibreglass. Thought is also given to the framework of a balcony, which is not so exposed to the elements as a roof terrace and is frequently treated more as a natural extension to the apartment than as a space in its own right.

The roof garden is now ready to be furnished, gradually or all at once, depending on your budget. Chapter 3 outlines the vast range of tables and chairs, loungers, umbrellas and containers that can be purchased from garden centres, trade shows and department stores, as well as catalogues and antique shops. It also looks at the smaller-scale furniture that would be suitable for a balcony. Ornaments of all types, and lighting, from fairy lights to uplighters, will refine and perfect the mood, and the gentle sound of water could be introduced with a carefully chosen feature.

The actual gardening element of a terrace high up in the sky might seem daunting. Which plants will be able to withstand strong winds without breaking or losing their leaves? Will it be possible to grow flowers for colour and

above *This well-established garden is a remarkable example of a retreat up in the sky where a completely secluded seating area can be so close to neighbouring buildings.*

opposite *The harmonious way in which all the elements have been used on this contemporary terrace prove that the emphasis on hard landscaping can bring elegance and diversity to a most inviting outdoor room.*

scent in summer? Which plants could be used to provide shelter for other, more delicate, plants? Chapter 4 suggests plants that are suitable for creating a barrier, making a statement, filling in the gaps and providing food, as well as giving ideas for plants suitable for a balcony. Plants that thrive in spite of gales and extremes of cold, for example those that grow in mountainous regions or on the coast, will probably be happy on a roof garden.

Finally, chapter 5, the plant directory, provides a listing of plants that could safely and successfully be grown in a roof garden, including trees, shrubs, climbers, perennials, annuals, bulbs, grasses and alpines. A description of each plant is given, together with details of its eventual height and width, its degree of hardiness and a little cultivation advice. A section on the practicalities of rooftop gardening provides all the information you need on planting and caring for your chosen plants in this exposed location.

chapter one

up on the roof

A roof terrace adds a whole new dimension to an apartment. Not only can it be thought of as an extra room, but it is set against a most extraordinary backdrop, where the crisp light of dawn or the blaze of sunset plays a starring role. Designing this fantastic space will be more like creating a stage set than a garden. While accommodating and paying homage to the natural elements, the main aim of the design is to produce an inviting space.

left This rooftop terrace, high above the bustle of the West Village, New York, looks out over the Hudson River. It provides the perfect place in which its owners can lounge, contemplate, and meditate.

planning a design

A roof terrace will become an important part of the life of its owners, whether it is a place for entertaining, a sunbathing haven or a retreat for quiet contemplation. The planning and design — whether formal or informal — will need to respond to the extraordinary nature of this confined space.

The look might be traditionally formal, with vistas and clipped planting in symmetrical arrangements that look towards France or Italy for their inspiration. A more modern version of the formal theme might adhere to the rigorous design principles of Japanese gardens, where the emphasis is placed on clean lines, the very precise arrangement of hard materials, such as large stones and gravel, and the choice and shape of trees and shrubs.

For a more informal look, sinuous lines and masses of colour can re-create a rural idyll, with plants bursting out of their pots, and plenty of seating for leisurely contemplation. Alternatively, a blue and white theme, with some suitably exotic planting, would give the illusion that the Mediterranean is just below, while tiles in terracotta, turquoise and red, as well as low tables and large copper lanterns with coloured glass panels, will conjure up a Moroccan setting.

Entertaining in this garden in the sky will be a delightful experience for hosts and guests alike. With far-reaching views and twinkling lights already supplied, the owner can concentrate on choosing the best garden furniture for the site, adding beautiful table linen and cushions to complete the experience of outdoor eating.

For more self-indulgent pastimes, the garden can be fitted with a sauna or hot tub – with accompanying deck chairs and loungers – while a water feature, such as a bubbling fountain or narrow rill, will provide the perfect atmosphere for calm contemplation.

If the outside space is a balcony, the pleasures and constraints will be slightly different. Here, size and aspect, rather than views, will be the determining factors. Partially enclosed balconies are necessarily intimate spaces, but they are also, by the nature of their added-on position, more closely related to their surroundings. Careful thought can, however, transform them into equally invaluable retreats.

above It would be difficult to find a more perfect combination than this beautifully furnished balcony overlooking the sea.

opposite The still water of this hot tub on a spectacular terrace in London's Docklands seems to be the perfect link between the river, the sky and the immaculately designed space.

right The geometric lines of this beautifully crafted furniture, placed with great care in front of an equally precise row of plants, contribute to a formal and elegant setting with a very contemporary feel.

symmetry and geometry

Through the ages and across the world, from Europe to Japan, formal gardens have depended on the principles of symmetry and geometry for their composition. Hard landscaping, with traditional materials, and symmetrical planting together create the backbone of the formal garden.

above *This inviting dining area overlooking downtown New York has used traditional design elements to great effect. The raised deck is backed by a box hedge and enclosed by a beautifully crafted pergola, with sculpted crossbars wreathed in immaculately pruned wisteria and clematis. An umbrella in the centre of the table completes the symmetry.*

traditional style

The evolution of garden design trends over the centuries has been underpinned by vigorous principles based on the constant aim of creating beauty through order and the use of a formal framework. The influence of formality is found all over the world, from ancient Persian gardens to those of the Italian Renaissance and the triumphant "French style" of the 17th century, with Le Nôtre, who planned the gardens at Versailles, as its most illustrious architect. The examples are numerous and well known, and even those gardeners who do not admire this strictly coded approach to design must acknowledge that it forms an essential part of our cultural heritage.

Aerial gardens are, of course, a far cry from the acres of Versailles, but the same rigorous approach to design can still be applied to great effect, since both types of garden are equally concerned with vistas, sky and horizons, and the unity of building and outdoor space.

A formal design is traditionally arranged symmetrically along an axis. In addition to ordering the plan, this axis leads the eye towards an important element or focal point, such as a statue or, when up on a roof, a feature in the landscape beyond. This link between the terrace and a view or landmark will take precedence over all other design considerations and will dictate the general arrangement of the space. The axis can be reinforced by using a contrasting pattern or colour in the floor material, so that the feet, as well as the eye, are led towards the focal point. In a formal design, traditional materials, such as honed or polished marble, granite or slate, will establish the scheme and give it the required elegance.

Classicists were masters at creating illusions of space. To give the illusion of spaces and a sense of order, we can follow their example by placing planters in rows along the axis or by using them in a geometric pattern to separate various areas, giving rhythm to the design.

Evergreens are the stars in formal gardens, with plenty of sharply clipped box, yew, Portuguese laurel (*Prunus lusitanica*) or privet (*Ligustrum*). Lavender and rosemary will equally lend themselves to being clipped while also adding scent and colour. If space and structure allow it, pleached trees will give instant grandeur, while espaliered fruit trees would give the same formal effect but on a more manageable scale.

above This remarkable roof garden in the heart of New York's West Village is laid out on two levels. This is the formal part of the garden, where rows of native inkberry (*Ilex glabra*) have been clipped into wonderful rounded shapes to form a most witty and unexpected parterre.

right Nothing in the arrangement of this split-level terrace has been left to chance. The precise geometry of the tall tapered pots, with their square cushions of box, sets the tone. The furniture is placed exactly at the centre of each space. Such attention to detail and the restrained choice of materials have transformed a difficult space into a very elegant terrace.

below Several elements of traditional Japanese garden design have been used here to create a simple terrace outside a modern building: from the stone lantern, large earthenware pots and dotted stones to the low seats and table, all backed by a bamboo screen.

modern style

Contemporary gardens are usually linked to buildings constructed of glass, metal or concrete. As a result, they rely heavily on hard landscaping and minimalist planting for their form and arrangement.

Japanese gardens, with their raked gravel courtyards, precisely placed boulders and clipped planting, have proved to be a perfect source of inspiration for contemporary designers. This is not, however, an exercise in re-creation but more one in deconstruction. What fascinates us about oriental gardens is how rigorously they are planned: each element has a symbolic function and a predestined position. The materials and the methods of building are strictly coded, too. This uncompromising approach was bound to appeal to those modern designers who wanted to go back to essential principles and a minimum of materials. It is also particularly suited to an urban context, as great effects can be achieved in very small spaces.

The flooring material used in a contemporary apartment is a very important part of its style and ambience. A good design starting point for the roof terrace is to extend the internal flooring material to the outside. Architects and interior designers make great use of limestone, unpolished marble and granite in penthouses, and carrying the same stone through to the outside gives continuity and sharpness to the design, as well as carrying lines of axis through both inner and outer spaces.

If the internal flooring is oak, the terrace can be decked in the same width of timber using cedar, iroko or balau. The area leading from the French windows (doors) or sliding doors to the far edge of the terrace should have the planks laid in the same direction as inside the apartment. To either side of this area – stretching out to both sides of the terrace – the planks could be laid at different angles, so indicating the separate areas of the terrace.

Repetition combines very well with geometrical designs. For instance, a row of large identical pots left unplanted will add decoration while also respecting the deliberately minimalist design. Large, freestanding stones or pieces of dark slate could give the same impression, as could a line of sharply clipped box balls growing in identical metal or timber containers.

Clean lines and a lack of clutter characterize the contemporary garden. In this context, furniture will have to be very elegant and simple, and placed precisely so as to emphasize the geometrical design of the terrace. Cushions must not be allowed to soften or detract from the crisp lines of the furniture, so plain fabrics and box-style cushions are preferable to chintz and frills.

above All the components used here are simple. A sheet of glass rests upon timber trestles, the seats are made of metal and timber, and the galvanized pots around the edges are filled with sword-like plants. Identical galvanized pots filled with small variegated agave, aligned on the tabletop, give instant sharpness to an otherwise relaxed space.

below This is another perfect example of rigorous design. Every element is rectilinear, from the treatment of the floor to the square cushion on the daybed and the precise alignment of the pots. The soft shape of the conifers in their black planters and the gentle curves of the tall clay urns reinforce this uncompromising design in the most striking fashion.

profusion and informality

Roof terraces are essentially urban spaces where harsh elements are often part of the decor. With careful planning and well-chosen materials and plants, however, the dream of re-creating an idealized vision of the countryside or a Mediterranean-style garden can be realized.

country-garden style

In complete contrast to the regimented design of formal gardens, country-style gardens provide a feeling of informality and bounty. This is best conjured up by massed plantings, established shrubs, rustic materials and plenty of places for relaxation.

For summer colour and abundance, the best and easiest route is to plant annuals. The great advantage of annuals is not that they achieve so much in so little time, but that by the end of summer they can simply be discarded: over-wintering is not a concern. For a while, annuals lost favour with gardeners, but they have made a triumphant comeback, often being planted in big sweeps. On the roof, this can be achieved by massing one type of flower across several planters. For instance, a colour scheme of deep orange and red would rely on *Rudbeckia* and *Crocosmia*. The blue palette could be represented by a great number of sages or by the lovely flowers of *Nigella* floating among a green haze of thin leaves. Colourful planting lifts the spirits and instantly evokes summer, and it certainly makes an impact with big blocks of a single colour and type of plant.

To complete the rustic illusion, a sympathetic floor scheme would use reclaimed materials such as mellow bricks in traditional herringbone or a basketweave pattern, limestone slabs or wide timber planks. Small creeping plants such as thrift (*Armeria maritima*) or violas could colonize the gaps left between the paving, adding to the feeling of profusion.

The most enjoyable way to relax in the sunshine in a country-style garden is, without a doubt, lying in a hammock. Beautiful freestanding hammocks – with a stand of either metal or curved wood – introduce a stunning ornamental feature while avoiding the problem of where to attach each end of the hammock. Loungers, deck chairs or wooden or metal benches piled with cushions and placed informally complete the relaxed ambience.

Although this type of garden is at its best in summer, it will still have winter appeal. Trailing ivy will soften the now-empty pots, evergreen shrubs, such as tall bays or *Viburnum tinus*, will mark out the structure of the garden, while the white trunks of silver birch (*Betula pendula*) will glisten whatever the weather. The first snowdrops peeping through in late winter will be followed by daffodils in spring and then all varieties of tulips continuing until the next summer.

above This secluded terrace, situated high up above the Upper East Side in New York, looks in on itself. The thickly clothed fences, as well as the mature trees and lush underplanting, contribute to a sense of peaceful intimacy in this informal dining area.

left The immense green "pool" of Central Park spread out below is the perfect foil for this spectacularly planted roof garden.

right Flowering plants climb up, tumble down, and peep through every available space on this vast rooftop terrace stretching over several low-lying buildings.

Mediterranean style

Instead of buzzing country meadows, you might prefer to be transported into warmer climes when sitting on your roof terrace. This could involve creating a Mediterranean feel – ranging from the African magic of Morocco in the west to Greece and Turkey in the east.

Roof terraces are very much part of the architecture around the Mediterranean, where they are often used as a place to sleep in the cool of the night or to rest or eat under some form of light roof. The colours chosen will play an important part: a combination of blue and white conjures up starkly white Greek houses against the backdrop of the Mediterranean, while terracotta and turquoise are more reminiscent of Morocco.

If the terrace is in a hot country, or if you are trying to create that illusion, the first thing is to erect some form of pergola with a roof to create shade. This could be simply made of thin metal uprights with wires stretched in between and covered with bamboo mats or lengths of linen. Thin, bellowing fabric could also be hung on the sides to give the feeling of a tent. A more permanent solution could be to build a timber pergola resting on fibre-glass pillars, draped with a grapevine (*Vitis vinifera*), a passion flower (*Passiflora*), a dazzlingly pink bougainvillea (*B. 'Miss Manila'*) or a deep blue morning glory (*Ipomoea purpurea*). Whatever is chosen, the play of light and shade is a very important part of this scheme, and this is encapsulated in the image of a grapevine-entwined timber pergola, under which there is a shady area for sitting and dining out of the midday sun.

In the shade, a white wrought-iron table and chairs, a day bed covered with a white mattress, or a wooden bench painted in a pale blue would reinforce the Greek theme. Another choice would be long, built-in benches with fitted cushions, which are almost a staple feature of all outdoor spaces around the eastern Mediterranean shores.

On the other hand, a Moroccan theme could be conjured up with large floor cushions in rich reds and ochre, rugs laid on terracotta tiles when the sun is shining, and low tables. A profusion of coloured glass lanterns or large torches would complete the picture. A dark blue and deep turquoise mosaic fountain would fit well into this decor, adding the gentle cooling gurgle of water as well as being a striking decorative element.

The planting is another essential factor. Though not all the climbing plants mentioned earlier are suitable for cool climates, there are many hardy plants that can create a similar effect. Aloes and agaves, with their striking, blue-grey, succulent spears, are the first choice for instant exotica. The New Zealand flax (*Phormium*), planted in a large Cretan pot, would give a similar effect. Some palms, such as the *Trachycarpus*, are evocative of warm climates and fully hardy, while bright-coloured geraniums tumbling over terracotta pots will always create a feeling of sunshine and profusion.

above What could better conjure up the essence of a summer day in the south of France than this traditionally furnished terrace facing the sun-drenched countryside under the cover of vines?

left The choice of colours on this sunny terrace, from the rich red floor tiles to the golden wall tiles and the posts painted a bright orange, has produced a very inviting space.

right By using elements associated with the Mediterranean, such as earth tones, terracotta tiles and exotic planting, this small urban rooftop has created a complete sense of place.

entertaining

Eating on the terrace is one of the great pleasures of having an outdoor space. With the ready-made landscape of the city at your feet, complete with glimmering lights, the roof terrace has to be the perfect venue for entertaining family and friends.

If cooking outside is an integral part of the pleasure of outdoor entertaining, then a barbecue will be deemed essential. Barbecues come in all shapes and sizes and different levels of sophistication. They can be built-in or mobile, they can use gas or charcoal, and they can also be disposable – the choice gets wider all the time. In countries with cooler climates, however, where the number of times one can cook outside is fairly limited, a simple barbecue may be best. A model on wheels, which can be easily covered up and pushed to one side in winter, or a beautiful Thai barbecue, which looks like a large terracotta pot when not in use, might be preferable to an elaborate brick construction.

If siting the barbecue is a problem, or if there are concerns about stains and grease marks on the floor, then the food could simply be cooked inside and brought out to the table when it is ready.

As part of the theatre that is a roof terrace, the food, whether cooked inside or out, should be served on the most glamorous table setting possible, and lit with lots of candles at night. If there is room, a large, well-constructed table is an asset and a worthwhile investment. Fitted with a stabilized canvas umbrella and surrounded by solid chairs, it creates an instantly inviting area. Some umbrellas can be bought decorated with fairy lights wound around the ribs, making this area the focus of life on the terrace whenever the weather allows, from breakfast in the golden light of morning, lunch in the shade to dinner at night.

It might also be a good idea to invest in a gas space heater. These come in a wide range of sizes, from table-top to large freestanding models, and they extend the use of a roof terrace when the nights get chilly.

On a warm summer evening guests will be immediately charmed by the sense of escape that is felt on a roof. Whether they have come to take part in a celebration or a family barbecue, the roof garden will offer an instantly glamorous setting whatever the extent of the views. The built-in backdrop of sky, city lights, stars and moonlight will not only contribute to the relaxing atmosphere, but also provide instant topics of conversation.

above *The same Docklands terrace (opposite) in daylight reveals that it is laid out for total entertainment. The carved wooden cubes for seating, the gleaming barbecue poised for use and the hot tub nestled among plants complete the range of possibilities.*

left *This well-designed small barbecue stands on gravel, which can easily be replaced if it gets stained by cooking. Stretched canvas protects it from the wind and defines the cooking space.*

relaxation and play

Away from the cares and noise of the world below, the roof garden is the perfect place for some rest and recreation. This could involve sunbathing in a quiet corner on a hot day, playing games with family or friends, having a sauna or maybe even soaking in a hot tub.

above left Even a small balcony can become an extra room in which to enjoy a cup of coffee, and maybe check your emails.

above right This lit-up sauna set in a timber building on a large roof terrace could not be more inviting.

For quiet moments away from the hustle and bustle of life, various "corners" of seclusion can be created. Consider a mismatched collection of antique chairs and colourful fabrics under a big umbrella; a hammock hidden behind tall grasses; a favourite wicker chair next to a climbing rose; or brightly coloured woven plastic mats and cushions on the floor, with low tables in Middle-Eastern style. In addition, deck chairs and loungers provide an invitation to sunbathe or catch up on some reading.

The terrace could also be the perfect place to keep up with letters or emails. Power and phone points can be installed to allow you to plug in a computer and connect up to the outside world. If music is part of the relaxing ambience, consider installing an outdoor sound system. These are becoming increasingly less intrusive, and there is a growing range of speakers available that are cleverly camouflaged to look like various types of rocks.

It might be a good plan to dedicate an area to game playing. The dining table would be an excellent place for board games, with shade provided by a large umbrella, but more energetic activities might be provided for with a basketball hoop fixed to the wall. It will take up

above This large daybed seems to symbolize the essence of summer. Beautifully crafted in timber, with wheels for easy manoeuvring, it is generously proportioned to allow for big, comfortable pillows and the placing of books or whatever else is required for total relaxation. The backdrop of agapanthus and fragrant lavender completes the experience.

little room but encourages some running around, though it should be sited well away from the parapet – any object falling from a rooftop would be extremely hazardous to anyone walking below. An outdoor-quality table tennis set is another possibility; some double up as pool tables for extra versatility, and they can be folded for winter storage.

If space allows, a sauna perched on the roof will provide another way of indulging in some luxurious relaxation. A sauna kit can be bought off-the-shelf. If the custom-made watertight hut it requires is made of timber and surrounded by white birches, it would give the illusion of being in a Scandinavian country. Alternatively, the sauna could shelter inside a metal-clad construction for a dazzling contemporary look. To complete the experience, a freestanding outdoor shower should be located nearby. Excellent ready-made models in different styles are appearing all the time.

Even more wonderfully indulgent is a hot tub. What could be more relaxing or soothing than lying in deliciously hot water, massaged by jets, and looking up at the sky, even on a grey day? The cares of the world simply melt away. On a starry night, with the lights of the city twinkling below, this will be simply magical.

contemplation

By its very nature, a roof garden is a very privileged space, conducive to much more than just entertaining or sunbathing. With its closeness to the elements and the outstanding views it offers, the terrace is the perfect place to spend some moments of quiet contemplation or solitary meditation.

above This tranquil scene spells peaceful seclusion. Comfortable sofas totally surrounded by profuse planting invite relaxed contemplation.

below right The mesmerizing pattern of this wooden deck and the beautifully smooth spheres could be the perfect starting point for some quiet meditation.

The best way to become an occasional hermit might be to retire to a custom-made hideaway. This could be a gazebo made of timber and trellis, a pergola wreathed with scented roses or a simple arbour covered in honeysuckle. Positioned to enjoy the optimum view of either the terrace itself or the panorama beyond, this hideaway would provide the perfect place to escape from the troubles of the world. The seating could be a bench or even a day bed for total relaxation.

The design of the terrace itself might be dedicated to calm contemplation in the same way that the Zen gardens of Japan follow a strict code of design and materials to lead their visitors to spiritual awakening. The terrace need not be a slavish reproduction of the designs of another culture, but it can be inspired by the abstract simplicity they achieve through their use of clear lines and a restrained palette of materials. The design could be linear, with different materials worked in bands from the outside in, such as stones, round pebbles and gravel. The planting could be restricted to just a few well-pruned evergreen shrubs, such as *Viburnum tinus* or a dark green pine, to bring calm and serenity to the smallest space. Clumps of steely blue *Festuca glauca* and the grass-like *Ophiopogon planiscapus* 'Nigrescens', with its nearly black leaves, would create points of contrast and interest.

Another important element often found in gardens dedicated to meditation is water, either still or flowing gently to evoke one of the essential foundations of life. The type of water feature used on a roof terrace has to be carefully chosen, since it is competing with the elements surrounding it on a grand scale: too large, and it could look as though it were attempting to outdo nature; too small, and it would look insignificant. A long thin rill would fit in very well, reflecting the sky to create a constantly changing ribbon of colour. A fountain with water bubbling over smooth pebbles or a shiny glass sphere could be placed in a secluded area to induce quiet reflection.

A serene oriental statue made of timber or polished stone, resting among grasses or placed on a stone plinth in the axis of a sitting area would be a good focus for peaceful thoughts. Softly lit at night, it would take on a magical quality and become the favourite destination of an evening stroll around the terrace.

far left and left *Discovering the beautifully contemplative face of this wooden figure nestled among the greenery, or coming across this highly polished small statue of the Buddha in another part of this remarkable roof garden, seem to mark the stations of a meditative walk.*

above *Reclining on a comfortable lounger, watching the constant movement of boats on the Hudson River while the sun goes down, could be one of the best ways to feel at peace with the world.*

left An inviting view of a conversation corner surrounded by flowering plants and backed by a screen of tall bamboo.

opposite top right This granite-topped table is next to the barbecue and can be used for preparation or for an informal meal. Built-in cupboards store the cooking utensils and crockery.

below The thought of playing basketball on a 10th-floor terrace might induce vertigo in some, but for the two teenage boys living here the hoop is very much part of life.

case study: *designed for living*

This wonderful terrace, perched high above Park Avenue in New York's Upper East Side, has been designed to accommodate all the members of the family, who love living outside most of the summer rather than fleeing the heat of the city.

The very large terrace has been divided into various areas while still keeping the flowing sense of one space. Some areas enjoy long views through an arch framed by plants, while other parts are shaded by a pergola or hidden by an awning. Views out are not so much the point here but rather the creation of a garden offering something ravishing to look at whichever way you turn. This luxurious space is really made for living.

The first area you step into resembles a vast entrance hall, giving an immediate sense of privacy and space. The building is wreathed in a profuse *Campsis* with bright orange flowers. The rest of the planting in this area is mainly green and white, with tall railings covered in climbers on top of the parapet walls to provide a strong backdrop while screening neighbouring buildings. A basketball hoop encourages the two teenage boys to run around, and the nearby outdoor shower helps them to cool off afterwards.

Then comes an area given over to relaxation, with solid timber loungers, and another to leisurely conversation, with a sofa, chairs and a low table under a large umbrella. All the fabrics are crisply white, including the umbrella, echoing the mainly white flowers in this part of the garden, where *Gaura* explode next to hydrangeas against the backdrop of a hedge of tall box. Generous bunches of roses in glass vases appear on all the tables.

Beautifully crafted trelliswork covers most of the walls and has been used to create a box shape which hides the air-conditioning pipes that serve the building. It also creates a slight recess for a large gleaming barbecue and a black granite table, while various ornaments add to the feeling of a room. Beyond a metal arch draped in bright pink *Mandevilla* is a more formal dining area under an awning outside the kitchen of the apartment.

At night the terrace is possibly even more extraordinary than during the day. Lovely fabric lanterns gently light the invitingly laid dining table. Candles are lit in blue, pink, or golden glass storm lamps or lanterns hanging from every possible branch and overhead structure. Light-sensitive copper fairy lights light up at dusk, while tall gas torches add yet another type of lighting to create a totally beguiling atmosphere on a silkily warm evening.

centre The solid timber furniture has great presence, and the crisp white cushions are in harmony with the mainly white and evergreen planting, and also the white umbrella, just seen.

bottom The table is beautifully set for an outside meal on a warm evening. The silk hanging lanterns have electric bulbs to complement the numerous candles and fairy lights.

left Cooking on this gleaming built-in gas barbecue with state-of-the-art controls could not be easier and certainly removes the anguish of getting the embers to the right temperature.

right This part of the terrace is completely enclosed by tall railings for safety and privacy in summer when all the climbing plants are growing, while still allowing views through.

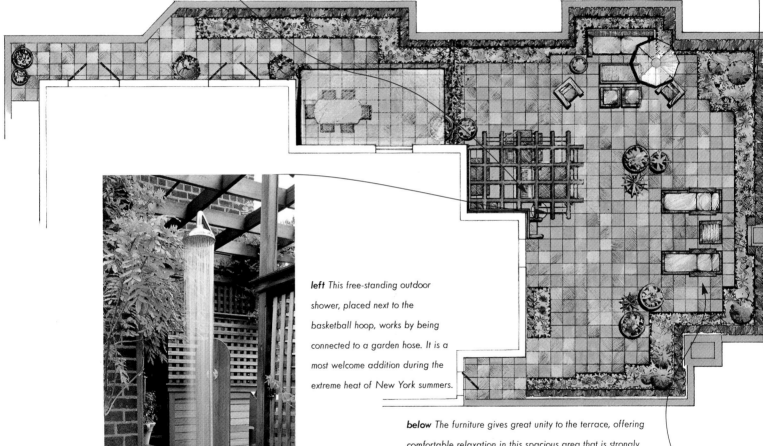

left This free-standing outdoor shower, placed next to the basketball hoop, works by being connected to a garden hose. It is a most welcome addition during the extreme heat of New York summers.

below The furniture gives great unity to the terrace, offering comfortable relaxation in this spacious area that is strongly defined and enclosed by a tall box hedge.

Building a pergola

Traditionally, a pergola is a simple covered walkway leading from one area of the garden to another in the shade of climbing plants. On a roof garden, the same principle can be applied to create both shade and a sense of intimacy for one space, often the dining area.

1. Choosing the spot

The increased wind factor on a roof terrace means that it is advisable to build a pergola only if some of the supports can be attached to a wall for extra security. For this reason, the instructions given here assume that one end of each crossbar will be fixed to the wall and the other will rest on an upright.

2. Choosing the wood

Cedar has long been a favourite for such structures, but some of the hardwood from renewable sources in South-east Asia, such as balau or kwilla, or in South America, such as ipe, are equally suitable. Oak is another excellent choice, since it is easy to work with and native to most Western countries. You must be aware, however, that oak pegs should be used to construct an oak pergola, as any metal screws will leave black marks. If a painted finish is preferred, a pressure-treated softwood such as pine can be used.

3. Planning the pergola

Mark out the area and decide on the number of upright posts required. These should be set at a maximum distance of 1.5m (5ft) apart. The posts should measure 15 x 15cm (6 x 6in), and the ideal height is 2.1m (7ft). Each upright post requires a galvanized plate, also measuring 15 x 15cm (6 x 6in).

For each upright post you will also need a crossbar measuring 15 x 7.5cm (6 x 3in) x the depth of the area you have decided to cover. The crossbars could end flush with the posts or be cantilevered on the uprights, although they should not project by more than one-third of their total length. Their ends could be cut straight or have a traditional curve to them.

4. Buying the materials

Buy the timber cut to size from a garden centre or builder's merchant, and also the galvanized plates. Hollow out one end

above *Immaculately constructed trellis-work hides the services while supporting the intricate pergola that acts as a roof over the cooking area. The structure is attached to the building and reinforced by metal tubing for strength.*

of each upright post so that it can fit on to the spike part of the plate. Cut the ends of the crossbars to the required shape, and cut a notch in the underside of each one where it will rest on its corresponding upright post.

5. Building the pergola

First, bolt the galvanized plates to the decking or tiles at the points where the upright posts will stand. Then slot each upright post on to the spike so that each plate is no longer visible. Next, bolt the crossbars to the wall so that their notches rest on the uprights. Finally, attach wires or thin metal tubing to span the spaces in between, forming a roof on which to grow any plants.

6. Finishing the timber

Hardwoods and cedar should be left untreated, because they will age to a beautiful silvery grey. Softwood should be stained with a suitable outdoor stain that will let the grain show through. The best colours to choose would be blue-grey or dark green.

7. Planting the pergola

Decide on the planting, and place pots at suitable points on the ground so that the plants can climb up the upright posts.

chapter two

the framework

With decisions made about the essential style

of the roof garden, now is the time to put

theory into practice and construct the

framework. Boundaries, offering privacy and

protection without compromising rooftop

views, must be chosen, floor surfaces selected,

and decisions made regarding any permanent

structures to finalize the scheme. These elements

provide the basic structure of the terrace, and

their importance should not be underestimated.

left This beautifully executed terrace provides a shady, minimalist retreat from the

heat of summer. It could be in any hot country, and the fact that it is actually in

London is proof of the skills of the designer.

first considerations

Creating the framework of a roof terrace is the first step on the way to having a rooftop escape from the cares of the world. Boundaries must be erected for privacy and protection, though without blocking desirable views; the floor must be surfaced, and any built structures should be put in place.

above Design has not been left to chance on this city roof. Every element has been strictly considered and used uncompromisingly, from the smooth black slate to the contrasting white pebbles and the underlining blue neon lights.

The construction of a roof terrace is, necessarily, a much more skilled and constrained enterprise than that of creating a garden on the ground. The condition and load-bearing capacity of the roof must be assessed, as well as the effectiveness of its waterproofing. The problem of transporting the necessary materials to the roof level must also be resolved.

From a safety point of view, the first consideration must be the boundaries of the terrace. If the terrace is being forged from a new space, there may be no barriers at all; if it is an old terrace, there may be only a low parapet. The height of the enclosing boundary and any permanent structure will be dictated by local building regulations, while the choice of materials will depend on many factors from design considerations to accommodating the elements. Once the terrace is contained, attention can turn to the choice of flooring materials. The range is vast – timber decking, natural stone, ceramic, quarry or mosaic tiles, and even glass or rubber – and the importance of the choice should not be underestimated, because the flooring will act as the anchor point for all the other design elements.

Built structures, whether for shade, for decoration, or for growing plants on, form the final part of the framework. From brise-soleils to classic gazebos, there is a choice to suit every design style and budget. The simplest construction can be transformed by clever planting: panels of trellis can look stunning when covered in climbers.

When designing a balcony framework, the most important consideration will probably be creating privacy through the use of screens. Flooring materials will also need to be chosen.

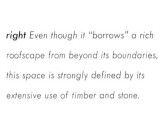

right Even though it "borrows" a rich roofscape from beyond its boundaries, this space is strongly defined by its extensive use of timber and stone.

below Simple wire mesh screens and well-laid decking are pleasantly echoed by the garden seat and the angular containers.

boundaries

The type of boundary chosen for a terrace will depend on many factors: opaque boundaries will provide privacy; translucent ones will give protection from the wind without blocking the view; arches can frame a focal point, and evergreen shrubs or trees can provide living barriers.

shelter and privacy

An existing low parapet wall will need to be raised to a safe height or replaced with a different kind of barrier. A very pleasing way to achieve both shelter and safety, while not interfering with the view, is to erect toughened glass screens framed in stainless steel. These, topped with a timber handrail, could be just the right height to lean on, or they could be as high as 2m (6ft) to ensure complete protection. Although costly, such screens are elegant and long-lasting.

To be efficient, a screen must, paradoxically, let some air through. Wind will bounce with full force against a solid barrier, battering plants and people nearby and defeating the whole point of a shelter. Screens should therefore be perforated or slatted. Alternatively, if solid panels are used, small wind gaps should be left in between them.

Cheaper and less durable screens can be made with bamboo poles, split willow or woven hazel. They will have to be replaced after a few years, but could be a good first solution and will introduce a natural element to a stark new design.

In recent years, metal has become a great favourite, and perforated metal sheets or woven wire mesh of varying opacity and thickness have been used in many new schemes. The metal can be galvanized to turn a soft, dull, silvery grey, or it can remain shiny, as in stainless steel. With its beautifully rich copper tones, corten (an oxidized metal) gives instant cutting-edge appeal to a design.

Even simple, utilitarian materials can be used, such as the green plastic ribbons stapled to timber battens used in plant nurseries. Erected around a stunning terrace full of exotic plants, they form a very light and beautiful barrier.

Translucent sheets of polycarbonate, looking best in milky white and framed in steel, provide a wonderfully crisp look and create interesting shadows, while clear sheets in a variety of colours provide shelter as well as decoration. A particularly exposed corner of the terrace could also be protected by stretched pieces of canvas in interesting overlapping shapes like taut sails.

opposite far left Here the split willow fence leads the eye outwards.

opposite above right Plastic ribbons stapled to timber battens are used to elegant effect on this terrace.

opposite below right This screen, made of hollow concrete blocks, each one filled with a red brick, has become a repetitive, contemporary artwork in its own right.

top Toughened glass bricks have been stepped to give privacy and shelter while allowing light and the green of the fertile planting beyond this balcony to filter through.

above The transparency of the glass panels used to shelter this terrace from the sea breeze is so effective that there seems to be no boundary with the sea front.

framing and living barriers

As well as being used to create shelter and privacy, the boundaries of the terrace offer the perfect opportunity for framing important features beyond or within it.

Timber, which has always been used for fences, can be used to great effect here. Strips of hardwood, such as teak, balau, ipe or oak, can be left natural or sealed to create a semi-opaque screen. The design may vary from planks of identical height and width to random-layered heights and widths, used to form panels that lead the eye to a landmark in the 'borrowed' landscape or a decorative element in the garden. Treated softwood, such as pine, can be utilized in the same way, but it looks best painted a soft blue to melt into the sky or a dark green to make its own statement.

With a reference to Japanese gardens, a perfect framing device could be built using two vertical posts, of either timber or metal, linked on top by a thick piece of wood painted in the deepest red. Bamboo would be an equally successful choice for such a frame.

Trellis has a long tradition as a decorative element used for framing a view or an object. It comes in various thicknesses and patterns and can be used to build freestanding elements, such as columns, arches or complicated panels combining various shapes. Painted dark green or blue-grey, it provides a very elegant backdrop to a more traditional garden.

To create a softer look, plants can be used to define the boundaries and give shelter. A very effective way to ensure privacy when sitting down without interfering with the view is to install shallow timber planters, filled with flowers in the summer and trailing ivy in the winter, on top of a parapet wall. Not only is the wall height raised to provide extra privacy, but the plants provide an interesting foreground to any view. These planters must be attached very securely to the parapet wall.

In addition to using plants to soften or beautify a boundary, there is no reason why they cannot be used to form the boundary itself, just as in a hedge in a ground-level garden. To create an efficient living barrier, evergreen plants are the first choice. Evergreen trees such as pines, yew (*Taxus baccata*) or holly (*Ilex*) in large timber containers will act as focal points, while clipped evergreen hedges, such as box, *Viburnum tinus* or rosemary (*Rosmarinus officinalis*), in long, galvanized planters or purpose-built raised beds, will be decorative as well as protecting more delicate plants. A gap between the planters could also be used to frame a view.

above *This wide metal arch is a spectacular feature, as it acts as an arbour over the dining area, supports a magnificent climbing rose and frames the view beyond this large terrace.*

left *This traditional Japanese gate and bamboo screen are framed by two vertical posts linked by a ladder formation made of bamboo lengths.*

right *This carved door has been backed by a mirror to introduce a visual illusion. This use of a mirror not only hides whatever is behind the door but also reflects the garden, so giving the impression that it extends beyond.*

opposite above *Panels of slender diamond trellis are framed by robust posts to create a strong screen and support a profusion of hanging pots.*

opposite below *Low planting, such as these spireas, is a very effective way of creating a first line of vision without obstructing the big picture.*

floors

The next question is what to put on the floor to satisfy looks, practicalities and budget. Timber, with its timeless appeal and weathered look, will be many people's first choice, but other materials, such as natural stone, tiles or paving slabs, or some of the modern alternatives, should all be considered.

above The different levels of this timber deck create various separate areas while giving a feeling of spaciousness. The beautiful silvery grey tone of the weathered cedar adds to the elegance.

right This newly laid patterned deck constructed with balau still retains its rich tone. To preserve this colour, the wood needs to be varnished or oiled on an annual basis.

timber

The main appeal of building a deck out of timber, apart from its beauty, is that, being a "floating structure", its weight is distributed evenly over the roof. It also hides any imperfections and, if constructed in separate sections, is fairly easy to lift should any problems occur on the roof itself. Timber slats are screwed down, not nailed, with brass or stainless steel screws to an underlying network of battens. This structural base is as important as the top layer and must be laid faultlessly, as it will determine the final pattern.

The increasing concern for the environment and the insistence of some organizations on using only certified timbers has forced suppliers to look for renewable sources where forests are properly managed. This has meant that cedar and teak are no longer the only woods used for decking, and previously unknown woods, such as balau and ipe, have appeared. Like teak or cedar, they take on a silvery grey tint when they are exposed to light and are equally durable. Some owners paint the deck with a sealant in an attempt to keep the initial soft pink colour of the wood. This does, however, darken the wood slightly and makes it look rather lifeless; it also needs resealing annually, or even biannually.

natural stone

If the structure allows it and budget is not a primary concern, stone is a wonderful material to use, as long as it is treated to be non-slip. The range of materials and their provenance are now so wide that there is plenty of choice.

• Marble from Spain or Italy is either polished or honed in a great variety of colours, from richest red to palest cream.

• Black, pink or speckled granite can be used in small setts measuring 5 x 5cm (2 x 2in) or large slabs of up to 60 x 60cm (2 x 2ft).

• Beautiful, but expensive, honey-coloured limestone from France provides a classic, timeless surface.

• Pink limestone containing amazing fossils and black limestone (both much cheaper versions) come from India.

• Dark, shimmering slate, either riven or smooth, comes from Wales or, more unexpectedly, Brazil.

• Wonderful jade-like green quartzite is quarried in China and supplied in sizes ranging from a brick to a slab.

• Loose gravel is economical, easy to lay, versatile and easily replaceable if it gets stained by food or grease.

above Black Indian limestone is immaculately laid here with no space between each tile to create a striking surface in perfect harmony with the black terrazzo pots and the dark metal frame of the timber bench.

middle The balau deck is edged with smooth black paddle stones (tumbled slate off-cuts) to add a mineral element to the composition. Note the perfect alignment of the brass screws.

bottom Chinese green quartzite – used here in butt-jointed brick size – is a wonderful material that shimmers in sunlight and looks like jade in the rain. A wide band of balau frames the paving.

tiles, paving, mosaic and bricks

In situations where not only budget but also weight have to be considered, tiles are an excellent choice of material. The range is vast, limited only by the fact that the tiles must be frost-proof and non-slip for outdoor use.

Ceramic tiles, mainly Italian, come in an infinite range of colours. They can be the softest pink with a marble-like look, plain dark blue or wonderful 1930s eau de nil. Black ceramic tiles could create the most strikingly matt surface, giving incredible depth and contrast to a modern scheme. Quarry tiles, with their rich, warm, terracotta tone, are also very popular. Tiles lend themselves to rich patterns and mixtures of colours, which could be used to mark out different areas on the terrace. They would be particularly useful in the barbecue area, as they can be easily cleaned.

Mosaic is one of the most beautiful floor surfaces one could use. Glass mosaic tiles come in ravishing colours and sparkle like jewels, but stone or ceramic ones are more robust. The patterns are infinite and their versatility means that they can enhance any design. Mosaic could be used to define various areas or to draw attention to a particular feature, such as a fountain or sculpture.

Concrete paving stones, once associated with badly laid pavements and ignored by the design world, have made a comeback, and can easily be laid straight on to the roof surface. They can be the standard grey colour, which will offer a neutral background to any design style, or mixed with granite or limestone dust.

For a more naturalistic, cottage-garden look, the traditional brick is invaluable. Its small size makes it very flexible and easy to use in different patterns, such as herringbone or basketweave. New bricks are available in various colours, from the dark blue engineering brick to the more traditional terracotta house brick, and have sharp edges. Reclaimed bricks are softer looking both in colour and outline.

opposite top On this elegant terrace, the quarry tiles are the perfect foil for the ornate French furniture and profuse planting.

below Rounded stepping stones are attractively set among cushions of thyme to ease the transition between the inside and the concrete paving of the terrace.

new materials

On a perfectly even and smooth roof, resin-bound gravel is a wonderful material. It is very light, gives a very clean, sharp look, is durable and is easy to walk on. Gravel is poured into a thin layer of resin, clear or coloured, and as the choice of aggregate is quite extensive, it is possible to create bands or swirls of colour. This is obviously a skilled job to be carried out by a certified contractor.

Perforated black rubber tiles make an unusual and very hard-wearing surface. They are also cheap and easy to lay.

Finally, what about the humorous new favourite: plastic grass? No longer confined to the vegetable stall, it is being used more and more outside. The colour almost replicates natural grass, the material is soft enough for bare feet, and it is durable thanks to its waterproof underlay and sprinkling of tiny rubber balls between the "blades". Even die-hard lawn-lovers have been known to be impressed.

far left Pebbles of various sizes can create a decorative floorscape, but only small resin-bound gravel should be used for areas to be walked on.

middle left The green artificial lawn, and the stool with its own cushion of fake grass, prove how comfortable and good-looking this material now is.

near left Randomly laid mosaic tiles in various shades of blue, with inserts of shells and glass beads, instantly evoke the seaside.

shade and shelter

The terrace now needs focus, definition and vertical lines. Permanent structures will complete the hard landscaping and play a very important part in the overall design. They will lead the eye from the building to the terrace, give shelter from the hot sun and provide decorative focal points.

opposite *This is the ultimate combination of shade and beauty. Made of cast iron, with a motif of vine leaves, it was installed when the tall building on which it stands was constructed in the early 1930s. It could not easily be replicated, but its dreamlike quality could not be more inspirational.*

below *Carved timber struts are fixed to the building and linked by metal tubing to provide a subtle transition between the inside and the outside. The luxuriant Campsis, with its orange trumpets, twines its way along this brise-soleil, acting as a natural canopy.*

linking building and terrace

The completely artificial nature of an aerial garden means it needs to relate to the building it belongs to even more than a terrestrial garden. To ease the transition between inside and outside, the brise-soleil is a very useful and elegant architectural device.

Its main function, as its name (from *briser* to break and *soleil* sun) indicates, is to provide shade to the interior, but, used well, it can also become a feature of the external design. Horizontal timber or metal struts project from the building and are joined by thinner pieces running parallel to the building. The whole construction can be very plain or quite ornate, depending on the style of the building. This introduces shadows as well as dappled shade and makes a very pleasing entry into the landscaping of the garden.

A brise-soleil can be left as a purely architectural element, but it could also be covered in climbing plants, such as a wisteria or *Campsis*, creating a garland around the building and giving it a luxuriant look.

providing shade

Light is much harsher on the roof, and a covered area will be most welcome to provide protection from the sun. Such protection could start immediately outside the building with a retractable awning made of canvas or synthetic fabric, striped or plain. Although it is a major investment, an awning brings a very welcome element of comfort and elegance to a terrace.

Traditionalists will love having a true gazebo on the roof, with a cupola, columns and maybe diamond lattice walls. This classic garden pavilion can also be successfully reinterpreted in a modern idiom using different materials and shapes. The framework could be constructed of slender metal posts supporting galvanized wires. In the summer, lengths of cloth or woven mats could be attached to this structure. Alternatively, strong canvas could be permanently stretched between the uprights and securely fastened to create lovely shapes. Timber posts holding a slatted roof will give an element of shade but no real protection from the rain. For true outdoor lovers, a solid roof would ensure complete shelter all year round. It could be made of wooden shingles or corrugated iron, which would add sound effects on a rainy day.

These constructions are obviously ambitious and, because of the extra stresses and strains imposed by the high elevation, should be built by professionals, who will also make sure that there are no planning issues involved. If a permanent shelter can be included in the design, whether it is a simple awning or an extravagant pavilion, it will become a huge asset, allowing the terrace to be enjoyed all year round.

structures for planting

While some permanent structures are designed primarily for shade, others are designed to be adorned with plants. Arbours, pergolas and all kinds of structures made from trelliswork provide the perfect showcase for climbing plants, as well as introducing an important vertical element.

Traditional wooden trelliswork is a safe choice for any structure, and extremely versatile. It can be custom-made into all possible types of shapes. Arches give depth to a long view while announcing a new area of activity. A succession of arches painted a pale grey-green could be covered with different plants, starting with an unscented climber, such as the bright orange trumpets of *Campsis radicans*, followed by a jasmine (*Jasminum officinale*) and ending with the intoxicating scent and deep red flowers of *Rosa* 'Guinée'.

Obelisks, pyramids and columns can also be made out of trellis. Painted dark green or black, they can form focal points and decorative elements in their own right, but they are transformed when planted with climbers inside them, so that the delicate flowers of *Clematis viticella* 'Royal Velours' or *Clematis campaniflora* peep out through the holes in the trellis shapes to make floral sculptures.

An arbour is a very romantic way to envelop a seat and conjures up the very essence of summer, the name alone being so evocative. It is a three-sided construction with a top that is entirely made of latticework and covered in plants, permitting a good view out but with some degree of protection. Scent is another important element, which is why arbours have traditionally been wreathed in powerfully scented roses, such as the pink *Rosa* 'Mme Caroline Testout' or the beautiful red *R.* 'Souvenir de la Malmaison', or sweet-smelling honeysuckle (*Lonicera*). As in the case of a gazebo, an arbour can be designed to fit into either a traditional or a modern scheme by using different materials. If made of slender, diamond-shaped trelliswork, and painted with a pale grey or blue-green wood stain, it will constitute a beautiful addition to a classic scheme. Conversely, constructed out of reinforcing rods or upright galvanized posts with tensile wires, or timber posts and struts, it would fit into a modern scheme with great ease.

A pergola has to be the ultimate structure to grow plants and to introduce an architectural element of great impact. In a terrestrial garden, a double row of columns supporting a canopy of horizontal wooden beams usually covers a path leading to a place of interest. On a roof, such a construction could be simplified to a single row of light fibreglass columns linked by wooden beams to define a dining area. The wooden beams could be used to support a wisteria, so that the flowers dangle through them. Alternatively, the pergola, covered in scented climbers, could lead towards a focal point or the best view.

above Lattice trelliswork is one of the classic structures of garden design. Here, long panels painted white and surmounted with ornate finials are in complete harmony with the mass of climbing and flowering plants on this bucolic terrace.

opposite The contrast of this idyllic rural arch against a backdrop of skyscrapers could not be more startling. Profusely planted with a tangle of Ipomoea and roses, it functions perfectly as a dividing frame, inviting you to push the little gate.

below In this very contemporary take on the traditional arbour, copper tubing has been used to support a mass of roses and keep the unity of tone with the bench, the pots and even the cushions.

balconies

Whether a balcony is solidly built of brick or concrete, or light and almost transparent; perilously cantilevered from the face of the building with glass parapets, or more traditionally finished with vertical metal railings, decisions will have to be made about boundaries, screens and flooring.

Although a balcony will not extend the living space in the same way as a roof terrace, it will still provide a valuable addition to the home, and one that can be enjoyed rain or shine, as long as it is suitably sheltered.

A balcony enclosed with a parapet wall to 1.2m (4ft) will give an instant sense of privacy and safety, virtually creating an extra room outside. This could be an extension of the main living room and could include materials that echo those used inside. For example, if the indoor room has a wooden floor then the balcony could be decked with hard-wood such as teak, or a treated softwood, such as pine, which is suitable for a balcony because it is not so exposed to the elements as a terrace. The wood could be painted to emphasize a unity of design with the inside.

If the balcony is part of a row of adjoining spaces, it is important to create further privacy with dividing screens. Beautiful screens can be made of sandblasted glass with a wonderful green tint through the thickness of the glass. Another popular choice is timber, used in strips or solid panels to create a fence. Suitable candidates are teak, iroko or balau, left to weather to a silvery grey, or treated pine painted either dark grey or dark green.

Woven hazel or willow hurdle, or ready-made rolls of split hazel or willow, are very pleasing and a fairly economical solution for a screen, though it will last only about five years.

A balcony with open railings should remain as transparent as possible, with nothing to detract from the clean lines and chosen materials. A timber deck, a pale limestone floor, which would give an impression of floating lightness, or a starkly black slate floor to anchor the space would all fit well.

opposite This balcony overlooking Auckland performs its function admirably. Wide enough to allow for comfortable dining, it is shaded by a remarkably designed brise-soleil, while spotlights extend its use at night.

top right Containers planted with tall bamboo and hostas furnish this balcony outside a bedroom. The railings have been covered with a bamboo screen for privacy, and a large bunch of white roses makes the space even more inviting.

bottom right This small cantilevered balcony, clad in timber and glass for privacy and comfort, is the perfect breakfast spot.

case study: *symmetry of design*

This roof terrace is one of five situated on top of what was once a telephone exchange. The original terrace, with blindingly white concrete tiles, open metal mesh partitions and amazing views of London – but no privacy at all has been transformed into a sheltered, more intimate space.

above The terrace centres on the strong pattern of the radiating deck, reinforced by the symmetry of the planting and a feeling of privacy within the split hazel screens.

left At night, candles in little glass lanterns create a soft pool of light for dining against the lit-up backdrop of the city.

This modestly sized terrace has been kept as one space, with no attempt at dividing it into areas. The symmetry of planting and hard landscaping creates a powerful sense of unity.

The symmetrical design of this terrace, which measures 9 x 5.5m (27 x 15ft), is a response to its central position on top of the building. The radiating octagonal design of the timber deck flanked by two short boardwalks anchors it firmly while also making it appear to extend into the adjoining gardens. The hardwood iroko planks have already turned a silvery grey and, being wider than usual at 15cm (6in), give great presence to the deck. An octagonal centre-piece of black slate completes the design and serves as a base to a round table and chairs made of metal mesh.

The deck is raised 10cm (4in) above a grid of beautifully laid smooth black slate tiles (40cm/16in square) that contain lovely swirling patterns in the stone.

The desire for privacy finally won over uninterrupted views, and split willow screens were installed over the mesh partitions. They have made a great difference to the wind factor as well as creating lovely shadows.

The planting is laid out symmetrically, and all the containers are in tones of grey. Silver birches (*Betula utilis*) in large, rectangular, galvanized planters mark the boundaries on both sides. *Phormium tenax* in square galvanized planters are placed in the centre of the openings that were left between the terraces to comply with fire regulations.

The deck is edged with vintage zinc dolly bins, used in the past for washing clothes. Planted with large lavenders (*Lavandula vera*), they have found a wonderful new role creating a fragrant hedge of purple flowers in the summer around the dining area. A tall pine (*Pinus austricata*) in the only black metal container acts as a focal point on one side.

A timber bench, with stunning views, is flanked by a large pampas grass on one side and a hosta and hebe on the other. The entrance to the terrace is framed by a row of grasses (*Pennisetum villosum*) in mottled grey metal pots, two types of thyme (*Thymus citriodorus* and *T. serpyllum*) in galvanized buckets and perennial *Knautia macedonica* in a dark grey terrazzo pot.

above right *The containers include rectangular galvanized planters, a black metal planter and vintage zinc dolly bins, all chosen to accommodate large specimen plants.*

right *Pale grey terrazzo pots beside a traditional timber bench are planted with Hebe salicifolia and Hosta sieboldiana — safe from the slugs that attack hostas on the ground.*

right The smooth timber, weathered to a silvery grey, takes on a very attractive sheen in the sunlight, blending seamlessly with the equally smooth black slate in the centre.

right This ribbed vintage zinc dolly bin, a utilitarian object from the past, has found a new life as a perfectly proportioned container for a large lavender.

left The alignment of the white trunks of the birches underplanted with hardy generaniums introduces a strong vertical element to define the edges of the terrace against the dark brown hazel fence.

right These deck chairs bring a splash of white among the various tones of grey and green. They are brought out to use for sunbathing on the lower part of the terrace paved with black slate.

Building a paved area with a raised deck

Using two different materials on different levels is the perfect way to introduce variety and mark out separate uses of the terrace, while giving the illusion of a larger space. The best way is to use timber for the raised area, as the supporting joists will easily form the required step.

1. Planning and building the paved area

• Plan the design on paper and work out how much material will be needed for each area. Mark out the area to be paved on the floor.

• Choose thin tiles (2cm/1in) for manageability and weight. The most suitable materials are slate (see below), ceramic tiles or marble, but they must be treated to be non-slip.

• Lay out the tiles to cover the area. Some tiles will need to be cut to fit with an angle grinder. Make sure that you wear protective goggles and follow safety recommendations when doing this. If you are planning on butt-jointing the tiles, which means that there is no mortar between them, you can position them close together rather than leaving a space. This will give a cleaner finish. When the whole area has been covered, remove all the tiles, putting them carefully to one side, making sure you remember where the cut tiles need to go.

• Lay a thin bed of 4 parts sand to 1 part cement for the base. Create a fall of 1 in 60 towards the drainage point to allow rainwater to fall away. Lay the tiles on top. For better adherence, and to prevent rocking, brush each tile underneath with 1 part sand to 1 part cement mixed to a wet slurry before laying it in place.

• When the cement is dry, apply a proprietary sealant to protect the tiles from any spillages. This also has the added bonus of bringing out their colour.

2. Planning and building the raised deck

• First work out the pattern for the deck, as this will determine the layout of the joists.

• Calculate how many metres of timber you will need for the joists (both the main supports and the cross supports, which hold these in place) and the slats on top. Choose pressure-treated timber such as pine for the structure, and hardwood such as balau, ipe or cedar for the top. The joists should measure 10 x 5cm (4 x 2in). Have them cut to the required length by the timber merchant.

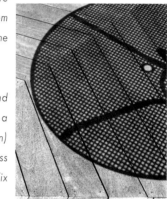

• Lay the joists out on the ground where the decking will be with a maximum space of 45cm (18in) between them. Nail the cross pieces in between the joists to fix the whole structure.

• The top slats specially sold for decking are usually 9cm (3.5in) wide, with one smooth side and one grooved one. The grooved side is anti-slip and is therefore intended to be the upper side, but this finish is less attractive than the smooth side and difficult to keep clean. In the end, the side you choose is a matter of preference.

• Screw the slats to the joists, creating a regular pattern. Brass or stainless steel screws should be used, depending on the final look required. However, it is important to note that only stainless steel can be used with cedar, as anything else will leave dark stains on the wood.

• The finish is again a matter of preference. Hardwood does not need to be sealed or varnished, as it will naturally weather to a silvery grey (see above). If, however, you want to keep the reddish tone of the new wood, you will have to seal it and repeat this operation every year, which you may not wish to undertake. If you do, there are some excellent oil-based products available that can be reapplied without the need to sand the wood down each time.

chapter three

decorative features

The scene has been set. Now is the time to make this pristine new space into another living area, whether it is to be filled with furniture and ornaments or left as empty as possible. The range of furniture and containers is constantly expanding, as new materials appear or old ones are used differently. Ornaments or statues can add character and focal points to the terrace, and exterior light fittings, which have developed a long way from the traditional spotlight, can transform the roof garden into a magical scene.

left This seating arrangement, evocative of the deck of an ocean liner, shows how simple wooden loungers can become decorative elements, particularly, as here, when they have turned silvery grey and are furnished with crisp white cushions.

the finishing touches

Furniture and decorative elements can now be chosen, preferably with some unity of style. Ideally, whatever is chosen should not be excessively ornate, since the most important decoration in a garden in the sky will always be the sky itself, with its ever-changing cloud patterns and breathtaking sunsets.

As with the hard landscaping materials, it will be important to consider questions of access when buying heavy items for the terrace, in this case furniture or large containers. Will they go through the apartment or in the lift (elevator)? Remember that furniture and containers have to be quite solid or they could be blown away by strong winds.

A further aspect to consider is storage. Can the furniture stay out all year round? If not, where will it go? Is covering everything with green tarpaulin in winter an acceptable solution, particularly if the terrace is entirely visible from inside? If not, new furniture made of totally weatherproof materials might be a more suitable option.

Unless one is very rigorous, the terrace can easily get over-filled. Most of us like possessions and are often unable to resist buying more pots and plants, or just one more orna-ment. For larger items, such as sculpture, there are the matters of weight and transportation to be considered when making a purchase. Will the roof structure accommodate a large stone sculpture? If not, alternative, lighter materials, such as fibreglass, which gives the illusion of stone or plas-ter, might be considered, but they must be secured safely.

Lighting this new space is a very important part of the design, whether you install a sophisticated built-in system or just use storm lanterns and fairy lights, or nothing more than simple candles in candlesticks or sheltered in glass jars.

Another aspect to consider is water, which has always been an important decorative element in gardens whether on the ground or in the sky. There are many new styles of water feature to choose from nowadays.

Finally, balconies will also need to be furnished, using even more forward planning to prevent clutter in the restricted space. You will have to use the walls, parapets and balustrades to create the decorative backdrop.

left At its peak, the splendid grass Pennisetum villosum *is the perfect counterpoint to this beautifully designed modern furniture made of metal mesh. The chairs are extremely comfortable, with the added bonus of casting very decorative shadows.*

above right *A shallow concrete bowl lined with shells and glass beads makes the simplest of water features.*

right *These classical urns form a striking contrast to the very modern black limestone and timber planters.*

furniture

Furnishing the terrace is obviously a matter of taste, but the design style set by the hard landscaping will doubtless be an influence. Beautifully crafted timber furniture will be at ease everywhere, but a bolder statement can be made through the use of contemporary materials such as steel or concrete.

classic furniture

Hardwood remains the favourite material for outdoor furniture. Teak is the most popular, but new woods from renewable sources, such as balau and ipe, are gaining in popularity. These beautiful woods fit in with most schemes, are heavy and weatherproof and require practically no maintenance.

Annual applications of teak oil will preserve the original colouring and protect it while allowing it to breathe. However, simply washing the furniture once a year with a light soapy solution and a high-pressure hose brings it back to its original beauty.

Oak is now being used more and more, and does look wonderful. Another possibility is to seek out eco-friendly pieces of furniture made out of reclaimed timber.

Whichever material is chosen, the first thing to buy will probably be a set of table and chairs. The catalogues of timber furniture are numerous, as are the showrooms and exhibitions to be visited before a decision is made. Make sure that the quality is excellent by looking not only at the wood but also at all the joints and fixings, as the furniture will have to sustain great stress from the rain and the wind. The comfort of chairs should also be checked. The table, and its matching chairs, is bound to become a focal point of life on the terrace, so buying one as large as the space will allow is a good investment.

Loungers and deck chairs are an essential addition to a roof garden, without forgetting extras such as little tables for a drink or a newspaper. If space allows, a row of them would instantly evoke a ship's deck or a seaside promenade in summer.

For a lighter, yet still traditional look, wrought or cast iron is a good choice. With its many curves and delicate volutes, painted white or a "faded" green, it evokes a French orchard at the height of summer. Cushions will be needed for comfort – delicate old-fashioned prints or checks, or plain, soft colours, will enhance the timeless look.

In a similar spirit, Moroccan furniture has made a big entry on to the garden scene, with black powder-coated metal stands supporting table tops of mosaic in muted tones. The accompanying metal chairs are usually slatted with curved legs. The matt black finish makes them look at ease everywhere. Adding Moroccan-style finishing touches, such as the tray, bowls and the ornate coffee pot shown below, completes the scene.

opposite above The colours of the cushions on this wrought-iron furniture fit in perfectly with the planting scheme.

opposite below The sturdy timber furniture with its dark green cushions is in perfect harmony with the building.

below left This inviting deck chair is surrounded by fragrant flowers.

below Both the table and the table setting have a Moroccan theme.

bottom The white umbrella provides shade and a "roof".

contemporary furniture

The design of contemporary furniture has come on in leaps and bounds, making the most of aluminium, steel, glass, plastic, nylon and even concrete. Wood, though usually associated with more traditional styles, has also been used to great effect by many contemporary designers.

Synthetic fabrics in deep blue or palest grey give a new look to very sleek metal deck chairs or ergonomically shaped loungers. Moulded plastic has been made into vibrantly coloured folding chairs, perfect for small spaces, as well as stacking chairs and even sofas.

Traditional café tables and chairs give an inviting look to an outdoor space. These have also been given a modern makeover, and the tables can be found in gleaming metal with black or silver synthetic tops, while the seats are made of woven plastic strands or a mesh of wide plastic strips.

Rigid metal mesh can be made into the most wonderful and elegant silvery dining sets, which have a much lighter look than their solid metal counterparts. A softer and finer version will give a beautiful shape to reclining chairs and loungers. A metal dining table with a glass or terrazzo top would enhance any scheme.

Lloyd loom furniture, with its beautiful woven paper strands, has been reinvented using man-made fibres to create immaculate loungers and armchairs on metal frames. These pieces, which are comfortable and stylish, will withstand some rain but should be protected in winter.

To create a truly contemporary look, the best item is undoubtedly a backless bench. Low and sharp looking, it will add a strong design element while not interfering with the general arrangement. There are some spectacular models on the market made of polished concrete, either solid or with a grid of perforations in the seat. The bench could be shiny or matt, dark grey or dazzlingly white. Fitted with a seagrass mattress, it turns into a most stylish day bed. Concrete stools, smaller and more manageable than a long bench, can double up as occasional tables.

Another kind of backless bench, roughly carved out of a solid piece of timber, such as oak, would become not only a focal point but a unique piece of art.

A hammock is the ultimate way to relax in a garden. The traditional version, suspended between two trees, will not be possible on a roof, but stylish free-standing hammocks, now available on sleek frames of metal or wood, are perfect for this situation.

Parasols are essential on a roof as protection against strong sunlight. As their popularity increases, so do their size and sophistication, and some modern versions have a stand located beside the table, from which a huge parasol is suspended over the diners on a large metal arm.

opposite top left Made of copper, this curved bench echoes the decorative sphere placed near it.

opposite top right The lounger has been updated by using a synthetic fabric on a very elegant metal frame.

opposite bottom Depending on the light, this curved glass seat with stainless steel legs will disappear or reflect the planting and the sky.

top right The shadows cast by this mesh chair add an extra dimension to the pattern of the deck.

right This weather-resistant modern woven armchair in a synthetic fabric is both striking and comfortable.

below left This freestanding curved frame is the perfect way to support a hammock on a terrace.

below right The rigid white plastic chairs complement a small metal table as an up-to-date café set-up.

containers

On a roof terrace, everything will be grown in containers, either free-standing pots or built-in planters. Pots and containers are now available in materials ranging from traditional timber to sleek sheet metal, and choice will be determined by considerations of weight, access and style.

left The dark grey terrazzo pots have been chosen here to echo the black limestone floor and the metal frame of the bench. Even the overflowing silvery grey lavender and the roofs beyond contribute to the unity of tone.

opposite top The determinant factors for choosing the stone pots on this wind-blown terrace were their weight and their agreement with the pale marble floor and antique spheres.

opposite middle A mixture of galvanized pots and low terracotta bowls are used to wonderful effect at the edge of this terrace.

opposite bottom left A row of identical galvanized pots placed on slate tiles and planted with variegated Agave give an instant touch of modernity to the glass table top set on wooden trestles.

opposite bottom right This simple container, made from concrete, is perfectly positioned next to an inviting deckchair.

free-standing containers

Large hand-made terracotta pots have been produced around the Mediterranean for centuries, and are still among the most elegant containers. Although very traditional, these pots seem to be at ease in any context. They are still made in the same age-old way, using a superb soft pink clay that weathers in great dark pink swirls. Machine-made terracotta pots are cheaper, but they are usually a strident orange and have little design merit, and so are better avoided. A row of Italian pots filled with tall grasses (*Cortaderia*), a pair planted with clipped box cones or a group with tall blue agapanthus, stately white lilies or annuals such as geraniums or white daisies (*Anthemis*) would enhance any scheme.

Crete has become another source of beautiful hand-made pots using a biscuit-coloured clay in various classic shapes, either ribbed or plain. An Ali Baba pot, for example, left empty but weighed down with stones or planted with a huge phormium, would introduce a stunning decorative element.

Another great classic being rediscovered is the Versailles case. It gets its name from the Orangerie at the Château of Versailles in France, where these large timber containers, hinged at one side to allow for plant care, were used to grow citrus trees and all sorts of exotics. Contemporary reproductions rarely have an opening side, and should be lined with a galvanized planter to prevent them from rotting. Their stately presence is sure to add a timeless element to any design. They look best planted with large specimens, such as a mature holly or a large palm (*Trachycarpus*).

When galvanized planters made of sheet metal first appeared, they were used extensively. Not only could they be made to any shape or size, but their muted grey colour fitted perfectly into the contemporary palette. However, thin metal can allow plants' roots to overheat in the sun, so planters should be constructed with good-quality zinc and have a double skin to protect the plants.

After being vilified for many years, concrete has made a triumphant comeback. It is the binding element in reconstituted stone pots, which are usually cast in a pristine creamy colour, in a great variety of shapes. If the budget allows, they can even be custom-made to an individual design. Starkly elegant terrazzo, where marble chips are mixed with dark or pale grey concrete, is the latest success.

custom-made containers

If the chosen design aims to give the illusion of a garden, it is possible to build planters directly on the roof slab, providing, of course, that the roof has been thoroughly inspected to ensure that it has sufficient load-bearing capacity and waterproofing.

One big advantage of custom-made planters is that they can be used to create the architecture of the roof garden in a more definite way than free-standing containers. There will also be no concerns, as there are with free-standing containers, regarding the danger of the planters blowing over, or even off the roof.

Planters are extremely versatile in their use. Arranged in a long line on either side of a length of decking and filled with clipped box, Portuguese laurel (*Prunus lusitanica*) or standard privet, they will form a stunning avenue. Placed in a rectangular formation and planted with a tall hedge of yew or box, they will form a perfect backdrop to a dining area. Alternatively, planters filled with lavender in the summer could separate a sunbathing area for privacy, with the added bonus of its soothing scent.

Once the area has been allocated, some form of retaining wall has to be constructed to hold the soil. The easiest way is to use reclaimed timber beams such as railway sleepers (ties), and then to line the planter with a permeable synthetic fabric. A layer of light drainage material such as Leca (very light clay balls) should be spread in the bottom of the planter, and then the soil placed on top. The depth of the soil can vary (30–70cm/12–28in), depending on the planned plant material.

For a crisper look, the retaining walls could be made of concrete blocks, which are then rendered. Several ancient techniques, with evocative names such as sraffito, marmorino and stucco, have recently found favour again with designers. These ornamental finishes are expensive, since they require the skills of a trained professional, but they will enhance any terrace by making the planters into more than just a functional part of the design. A range of textures can also be created by adding various aggregates to a mortar base, and yet more variety can be introduced by adding coloured pigments to produce unique tones.

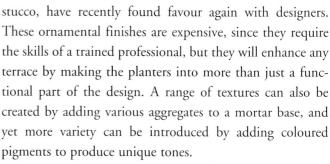

A more elaborate solution would be to build self-contained fibreglass planters faced with sheets of zinc or copper. The metal surfaces will mellow with age, turning to a dull grey or a vivid green. The dark green of a yew or a bay (*Laurus nobilis*) will marry very well with the grey zinc, while great sweeps of dark orange rudbeckia would certainly attract attention in a green-weathered copper planter.

Another possible finish would be to clad the planters with vertical lengths of natural hardwood or stained softwood. A group of these planters arranged in varying heights, covered by trailing ivy or the prolific tiny-leaved *Muehlenbeckia* and filled with several large phormiums or a mass of lush ginger (*Zingiber*), would replicate the feel of a luxuriant garden.

opposite top *This planter has been built on to the terrace out of rendered concrete blocks. It has been waterproofed with thick rubber sheeting and drains into a gulley along the back.*

opposite bottom *This low planter seems to announce the seashore it looks on to with a collection of succulents growing in free-draining pebbles against a protective glass screen.*

right *This splendid Japanese maple (Acer palmatum) has plenty of root space in a custom-made deep wooden container, neatly surrounded by shallower planters.*

below left *A series of galvanized planters has been specially made and arranged symmetrically on the edge of this terrace to form a long bed.*

below right *This deep wooden trough has a galvanized liner and has been painted a subtle purple-grey in perfect harmony with the mainly grey and maroon planting scheme.*

right decorative elements are successfully combined here, from gnarled beach wood to a specially commissioned group of metal figures perched on stilts, by Peter Burke.

below This row of stunning 1m (3ft) tall clay urns, designed by Luciano Giubbilei, are hand-thrown in Belgium and are raised on a zinc plinth to make a striking statement without any need for plants.

ornaments and sculpture

As the terrace becomes more and more a part of the life of its owners, it will evolve and be filled with objects that reflect their taste or current passions. However, although the ornaments and sculpture may come from many different sources, it is important to try to keep some unity in the design.

ornament options

The simplest items can be used to decorate and bring character to a roof garden, so there is no need to spend vast sums of money on designer pieces. Rocks or shells, memories of happy holidays, can be placed on a table or grouped on the floor to be endlessly rearranged as desired. Pieces of bleached wood brought back from the seaside will not be out of place so close to the elements, and will become a striking natural focal point. All sorts of objets trouvés can be used as decorations, although overdoing this could make a terrace start to look like a flea market.

Containers are often so beautiful that they can be used as ornaments in their own right. A single tall earthenware oil jar, for example, is so striking in its elegant shape that it does not need to be filled with any plants.

Empty containers in groups can also be very effective. Strictly aligned, a row of unadorned, starkly shaped containers made of unglazed clay or dark grey terrazzo could appear as a modern take on the traditional colonnade and be used to divide a dining area from a sunbathing corner, while a group of classic terracotta amphoras, arranged geometrically as a centrepiece, would introduce a shock element in the middle of a very modern scheme. The substantial thickness of the clay used for Chinese pots, as well as their generous rounded shapes glazed in shiny cobalt blue, carmine or deep turquoise, would enhance any monochrome planting, such as phormium or a group of lush grasses.

Reflecting the sky would be another spectacular way of contributing to the often surreal nature of the terrace. This can, of course, be achieved with water in some form or other, but a large metal bowl or a glass tabletop would have the same mesmerizing effect.

For a formal, classical look, ornaments made of stone, either natural or reconstituted, are hard to beat. A large, decorative vase, an obelisk or a group of perfectly round balls will bring an element of grandeur to the terrace. Modest stone ornaments can also fit beautifully in an informal cottage-type garden.

top *This giant shell, by the sculptor Hamish Mackie, brings an unexpected element to a lush planting of grasses and palms.*

middle left *These two birds are wittily perched on a small shed roof above a terrace, apparently making a short stop during their flight.*

middle right *These two wonderfully meditative heads resting on wooden plinths give you the feeling of having suddenly discovered a secret shrine.*

above *This copper fish, designed by Nigel Cameron, has been created as a wall sculpture fixed to a corrugated iron fence.*

using sculpture on the roof

Stone statuary placed as though in a terrestrial garden does not often work in a roof garden, since the figures look rather incongruously as though they had just dropped from outer space. Used wittily, however, they could introduce just the right amount of baroque decoration either placed prominently as a bold gesture or, more discreetly, just seen behind swathes of perennials or peeping around a large shrub.

If there is to be a piece of sculpture on the roof, it might be tempting, if the budget allows, to buy or commission an original work rather than buying a mass-produced object from a garden centre. Visiting art school degree shows is a very good way of getting familiar with contemporary trends and finding more affordable work by artists at the beginning of their career. Whether the work of art is to be the starting point of the design or just one among many components, it is important to have a clear vision of how it will fit into the overall scheme before commissioning it.

When deciding on the size, remember that the vast sky surrounding the roof garden can make too small a sculpture seem almost meaningless, unless a small piece is chosen to be the centrepiece of an intimate area of the garden. If you want a heavy sculpture, you must first check that the area of roof where it will go is strong enough, and get it reinfoced if necessary – bearing in mind the additional weight of any plants.

Statues and sculptures come in a range of materials. Stone, metal and concrete are all both visually and structurally strong. If the sculpture needs to be lightweight, a small piece in one of these materials may be possible, or a metal piece that is large but not solid. Lightweight fibreglass and plaster are less convincing for classic replicas, but can still be very effective in many cases, for example in this situation they would be invaluable for creating wall sculptures (as in the photograph opposite).

lighting

The importance of lighting should never be underestimated. Used clumsily, with unimaginatively placed spotlights, it can make the terrace an area of harsh light with no relaxing atmosphere. Used cleverly, however, with subtle washes and unusual shadows, it brings unforgettable magic at night.

above In this well-thought-out lighting scheme, concealed recessed uplighters create an inviting ambient glow, while visible fittings put a row of beautiful urns firmly in the spotlight.

opposite top Light is working its magic here by altering spaces and distorting scale. This miniature glasshouse, brilliantly lit from inside, is filled with plants and provides a focal point at the end of a path framed by shrubs and trees, all lit from the base on this vast roof terrace.

Built-in lighting will be an expensive exercise because it has to be installed by a qualified electrician, but it is still well worth considering because it will totally transform the space. It has to be worked out at the construction stage so that all the cables can be hidden under the finished floor surface before it is laid, be it decking, tiles or paving.

If ideas are required, it is possible to hire the services of a lighting designer, who will offer invaluable advice on how to create a mood while accenting certain features of the terrace, such as tree trunks, foliage or a sculpture, "washing" a wall with soft light, indicating a route or lighting up a dining area. Showrooms, where whole ranges of different lights are displayed, are good places to visit, as are the numerous garden shows, where there will always be people on hand to give excellent advice.

Spotlights are very versatile, and can be adjusted to illuminate a dining area or arbour, or to emphasize a display of pale flowers. (Take care not to place them too close, though, as plants can become scorched.) Spotlights are now available in many elegant styles, such as a small copper umbrella or free-standing granite or timber post, which will be at ease in any surroundings.

outdoor lights

In the past few years, the range of outdoor light fittings has greatly increased, and the most beautiful, tiny, low-voltage lamps, which produce a very atmospheric golden glow, are now available. They will transform any roof terrace with their subtle light.

Uplighters are useful to mark out a space or to indicate a route, if set into paving or decking. They can be used to emphasize a particular feature, such as a sculpture or the white trunk of a birch (*Betula*), while projecting great shadows from the branches. They can be placed in a planter to underline and throw into prominence the contours of the plants, and they can even be used underwater to create luxurious effects in rills and fountains.

Downlighters will accentuate the texture of a wall or the latticework of a gazebo. Installed on the building, they could work in conjunction with the interior lighting to create different planes of light, leaving the terrace back-lit for more drama.

Rectangular shielded lights fixed into steps will indicate changes of level – a vital safety feature if people are moving around the roof terrace in the dark.

right Recessed lights can have many functions: they can provide decoration while indicating a route, as with this pink LED (right); they can give diffused light to mark a change of level, as with this brick step light (centre right); or, as waterproof fittings, they can enhance water movement, as here, showing the ripples of a small cascade (far right).

above The magical effect of this curtain of fairy lights against the dark willow fence works perfectly with a row of small candle-lit lanterns placed symmetrically below.

below Tiny lanterns are wrapped around a metallic arch to make an enchanting entrance to another part of the terrace.

opposite top This hanging downlighter, which is encased in a perforated metal cylinder, directs a soft glow and gives a twinkling effect when moving in a gentle breeze.

opposite centre It is difficult to equal the charm of this lovely lantern with its golden glass shield and pink candle burning inside.

opposite bottom Fairy lights are no longer confined to small white bulbs, as this very pretty flower demonstrates.

opposite right The eerie light of this terrace accentuates the strikingly modern design with a very successful combination of spotlights diffused by glass bricks, a roof of fairy lights and the constantly changing patterns of the illuminated panels.

new developments

Most of the fittings used in gardens and on terraces take low-voltage or halogen lamps, which give a much richer glow than ordinary lamps. They have not, however, totally solved the problem of heat, which can be dangerous to bare feet, small children or plants, but an answer is now at hand: LED (light-emitting diodes), a revolutionary type of lighting already 20 years old but only recently making a big impact. The specification reads like a dream: up to 100,000 hours of life, low voltage, very low energy consumption, no heat and lots of colours to choose from. Inevitably, they are more expensive per unit initially, but they will hardly ever need to be replaced, and give a very soft light.

The world of outdoor lighting is abuzz with the new phenomenon of fibreoptics. Here the light of a single central lamp is "projected" through a system of mirrors along a network of wires. A tiny prick of light, white or coloured, appears at the end of each wire. These little dots will not actually give out light but should be thought of as light shows or fireworks. There are no restrictions to the configuration of the wires, allowing for the most wonderful displays to complement other lighting schemes.

back to basics

In addition to this built-in framework, or instead of it for a more natural look, candlelight is the most soothing and flattering light and so easy to install. In addition to their timeless charm, candles have the attraction of coming in so many different shapes and sizes, from tiny tea-lights to giant altar candles as high as 1.5m (5ft), which will cast an incandescent glow for many hours, with every shape, colour and size – not to mention scent – in between. To create an enchanted atmosphere, candles placed in multicoloured glass lanterns can be hung from branches, trelliswork or a pergola.

For a special celebration dinner on the roof, hundreds of tea-lights in glass jars could festoon the top of a wall or form an avenue to guide diners to a table lit with candelabra

or storm lamps.

For a more exotic effect, huge red paper lanterns could be used to evoke oriental delights, while delicate wrought-iron lanterns hung with coloured fabrics would conjure up Moroccan nights.

Finally, fairy lights, which used to be brought out of their box for the festive season only, are now being used by the most sophisticated of garden designers. Draped into delicate curtains, or made into long strands, they are perfect for enhancing a feature or outlining a tree, and can also act as the perfect backdrop to a dining area. However they are used, they project the softest light and instantly provoke smiles.

water features

The vast skies, swirling clouds and glowing sunsets, not to mention rain, that surround a roof terrace might provide enough exposure to the elements for some people. For many, however, water, and particularly the sound of water, is the finishing touch to the perfect garden.

Up on the roof, scale is crucial if water is to have any meaning and not appear as an after-thought. This does not mean that any water feature chosen has to be large, but it does mean that a small feature will need to be marked out in some way – surrounded by plants, for example, or defined by a striking floor pattern – in order to claim its role as part of the scheme.

fountains

There are numerous ways of creating that most popular of water features – a fountain. Surprisingly, no plumbing is required, only an electrical supply to a pump that re-circulates the water from bowl to spout and back again. This apparently simple and inexpensive construction has certainly helped to create the current craze for water features. No longer is the fountain something grand and sophisticated to be seen only in public gardens: now everyone can have one, however small their space.

It is important to stress that once the fountain has been installed, and the system tested to make sure that everything is watertight, some effort will be needed to keep the water clear and the pump working efficiently. Sunlight generates algae, which will cloud the water into a very unappealing green colour. This could block the pump, as might dead leaves and other debris. Simple maintenance and regular cleaning, as well as the addition of proprietary chemicals, will keep the water clear.

Despite the plethora of ready-made fountains, and the over-enthusiastic use of water features by many garden designers, it is still possible to introduce water to a garden in a tasteful and innovative way. Indeed, many outdoor furniture suppliers have realized that there is a great demand for such features and have added them to their range: shallow concrete bowls with a simple spout, shiny metal spheres pierced at the top so that water can gently run down the sides, or large pebbles in a stone container with water bubbling over.

As an adaptation of the fountain idea, a free-standing glass or Perspex screen, or a sheet of stainless steel or copper, could be placed near a wall or backed by planting. A pump could push water up behind it and let it sweep gently down the whole surface at the front like a slow-moving waterfall. With some subtle lighting, this could create a magical effect at night.

opposite middle right The slit-in-the-wall fountain is one of the recurrent features of modern garden design, and it is very striking when, as here, the free-standing wall is made of metal, and the sheet of water is perfectly symmetrical.

opposite bottom right A shallow bowl made of pale concrete filled with water and lined with shells, glass beads and slate chippings has been fitted with a small spout to form a simple and elegant water feature.

below left Water can make its presence felt in the smallest space, as this interesting self-contained fountain shows. A concrete bowl has been painted silver, set in a black concrete block and fitted with a spout to create a very precious-looking feature.

below Roof terraces are often surrounded by downpipes, so a good idea is to make them part of the décor, as rainwater gushing out of this lion's head into a hopper vividly demonstrates.

opposite left The sheet of water emerging from a metal frame and cascading down a series of glass steps is a very striking way to link the two levels of this terrace while providing the constant sound of moving water.

opposite top right Water feature designers are constantly searching for new ways of making water the centre of attention, as shown here by this mesmerizing swirling vortex in a glass sphere, designed by Bamber Wallis, placed on a stone table.

below and bottom *Here are two examples of rills that are both equally effective on roof terraces of very different scale. The small feature, with its bright blue mosaic tiles, fits neatly in the corner of the deck, making use of the difference in levels to house the pump. On the large roof terrace, the grander design aims to create as natural a landscape as possible, as if the rill, a shallow, rigid plastic trough, eventually ended in the river below.*

opposite above and below *Here are two possible ways of integrating a hot tub in the design. The large blue tub encased in metal has been cleverly positioned to make maximum use of the riverscape beyond, giving a feeling of vast open space reinforced by the seaside planting, whereas the round cedar hot tub, with its beautifully made ladder and sitting shelf, is a more traditional design evoking Japan. The new pale wood will soon darken.*

rills and tanks

If weight and budget allow, more ambitious water features can be built on the roof. A shallow rill made of metal or waterproofed timber faced with mosaic can run along the length of a terrace. It could be flush with the paving, and a gentle recirculating flow would create a playful feature to divide the space or jump across it. In a stricter geometrical interpretation, it could conjure up Persian gardens, or, flanked with tiny jets, evoke the Alhambra in Granada, Spain. Alternatively, the rill, instead of being self-contained, could lead to a shallow pool, either rectangular or square. It would be a wonderful mirror for the sky and a perfect place for quiet contemplation, as well as an occasional paddling pool on warmer days, though children should always be monitored when in the area, because even the shallowest water can lead to drowning.

A fibreglass tank at least 50cm (20in) deep and faced with stainless steel can be custom-made for the garden and placed in a premium position to create a perfect fish tank or lily pool. Surrounded by mosaic tiling and accompanied by dramatic planting, this would create a stunning focal point made all the more glamorous at night by the addition of underwater uplighters.

hot tubs and swimming pools

In the last few years, hot tubs have caught the imagination of roof terrace owners and developers. They are expensive and require a structurally sound base and strict maintenance, but they are certain to give hours of relaxed pleasure even in cold climates under grey skies. There are various models: the Swedish type, made entirely of cedar; mosaic-tiled domestic spas or even the soft PVC version, which has the great advantage that it can be emptied and stored when not in use. Without its cover, and when the jets are not in use, a jacuzzi can become a perfect reflecting pool, usually encased in a timber podium for sitting on. Surrounded by flowering plants or crisp evergreen shrubs, it becomes an irresistible attraction on the terrace.

The ultimate water feature, however, has to be a swimming pool: a fantastic way to introduce water on a roof. This is not a new thing on the roofs of New York, where many bright blue rectangles can be seen from above, but as a facility on a private terrace they are still quite rare.

features for balconies

Stepping on to a balcony, whatever its size, is exciting. The apartment is instantly extended by its presence, and there is a strange feeling of being outside yet inside. In the summer, this outdoor room will come into its own as the perfect place for meals and relaxation.

A little balcony outside a bedroom is the perfect place for a leisurely breakfast. A small round metal table with two slatted chairs, evocative of French cafés, would be a very good choice here. They could be painted a pale blue-green or left silvery grey for a more contemporary look.

A larger balcony outside the main room could accommodate a rectangular wooden table flanked by backless benches. These would use less space than chairs but still allow for friends and family to eat alfresco. A small table barbecue would complete the outdoor experience.

Folding deck chairs are a good addition on a balcony, whether they are made of wood with a canvas seat in either white or the traditional colourful stripes, or of light aluminium with a synthetic mesh fabric in pale grey or dark blue. If there is room, even a day bed ready for a siesta could be a most inviting feature on the balcony. Made of either metal or wood, it could be covered with a white mattress and lots of colourful cushions.

Adding decorative elements, such as sculpture and ornaments, is more difficult within the restricted space of a balcony. The wall space could, however, be used to hang a piece of sculpture, or glass privacy screens could be etched with specially commissioned designs.

Containers can be added to the balcony to make it into a miniature garden. There may not be much room for pots on the floor, but the boundary, whether a parapet wall or open railings, can be used to introduce plants. Long, shallow troughs can be anchored securely on top of the wall or fixed through the railings, then filled with suitable plants for a summer-long display.

opposite The floor of this well-designed balcony has been decked for comfort, and the space is big enough to sit and look at the view through a transparent balustrade.

above right An ornate metal stand supports a magnificent arrangement on this balcony. There is no shortage of sunlight here, but on balconies with high, solid walls, raising containers on stands is an elegant way to give plants more light.

right The choice of a single tone of blue paint for the cylindrical planters and the chair on this balcony has made them into a striking feature.

case study: areas of pleasure

This stunning terrace wraps around a sunroom on the tenth floor of a recent development in London, with panoramic views over the Thames. The creation of separate areas, all well sheltered and designed for different activities, has prevented the large terrace from feeling exposed and bare.

Entertainment and relaxation are the order of the day for the owners of this terrace, and a combination of an eating area, a jacuzzi and sauna, plus a cedar sundeck with plenty of seating, make this the perfect place in which to unwind.

The sunroom, which has a limestone floor, leads on to the adjoining terrace, which is divided into three distinct areas by means of two elegantly curved screens made of metal mesh and angled from the building.

The central section is easily accessed from the stone spiral staircase that leads up from the floor below, and this is the first area into which you step from the sunroom. Paved with pink Italian tiles and furnished with black Moroccan wrought-iron tables and chairs, it is the area set aside for entertaining. The muted pink and cream mosaics of the tabletops echo the colour of the paving as well as the terracotta pots along the parapet wall.

On either side of this paved area are raised cedar decks. The deck on one side has rows of wooden loungers and small tables, with a wooden hut housing a sauna at one end. The other deck is given over to a jacuzzi lined with green mosaic and encased in a stunning, circular, custom-made wooden podium. The whole effect is reminiscent of an ocean liner.

The final area of the terrace is the top of the sunroom, which can be accessed by a small staircase and is completely dedicated to the breathtaking views. It is furnished with only a table, a few chairs and, of course, a telescope.

The terrace is frequently used in the evening, and so the lighting is an important part of the design. There are built-in lights to illuminate the tables from above, to mark the change of levels between the areas and to lead to the jacuzzi and the sauna; they also enhance the planting and the walls of the building.

The planting is restricted to species able to withstand the strong winds. Both decks are outlined with plastic troughs faced with woven willow and planted with tall eucalyptus to give some privacy. Feature points are created by Cretan pots filled with rosemary (*Rosmarinus officinalis*) and lavender, while two trees – an olive (*Olea europaea*) and a bay (*Laurus nobilis*) – have survived well against the shelter of the building in beautiful Ali Baba pots. The hot tub itself is festooned with box balls and the grass-like *Liriope*, which complement the bleached timber of the surrounding podium.

The dining area is slightly more formal. Box pyramids in dark grey Versailles tubs frame the area, and a line of large Italian lemon pots, planted with pampas grasses (*Cortaderia selloana*) swaying in the wind, forms a spectacular barrier against the wind.

opposite left The design of the indoor and outdoor spaces is seamlessly linked by a lightness of touch in both cases.

opposite right This magnificent hot tub is the star here, as its dramatic position in the centre of the deck unequivocally announces.

below The dining area of the terrace is paved with ceramic tiles in earth tones. The huge pampas grasses give some protection from the wind.

right To keep the pampas grasses healthy in their containers and to avoid a pyramid of dead leaves forming in winter, they should be cut right back in autumn.

right The row of wooden loungers on the sundeck, with the Thames below and the vast expanse of sky above, invites relaxation before or after a sauna.

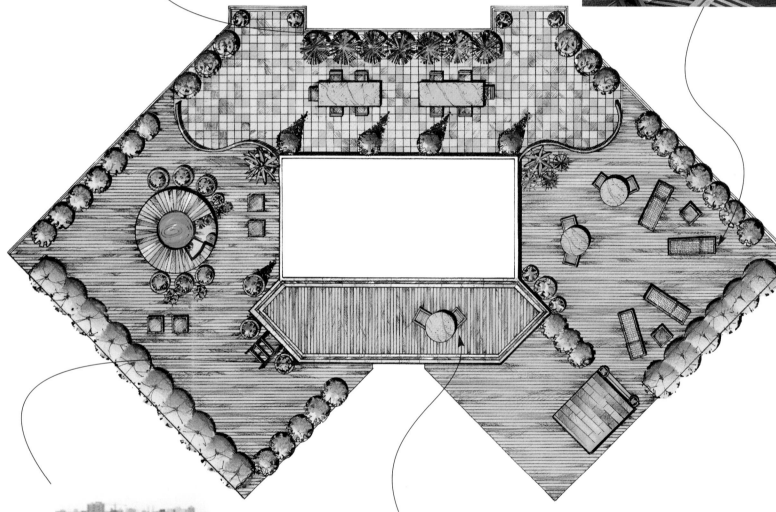

left A well-designed powder-coated metal frame is fitted with sheets of toughened glass for a very efficient and transparent balustrade to the viewing deck. A small gap deals with the sharpness of the corners.

left The viewing deck above the terrace is accessed by a small staircase and a bridge. Apart from a café table and two chairs, this area has been left uncluttered, as the panoramic views need no adornment.

Planning a lighting scheme

There are so many types of outdoor light now available that your lighting scheme will constitute a major part of the design. Getting the scheme just right can make all the difference between a garden that feels rather cold and uninviting, and one that is completely enchanting.

1. Planning the lighting

Decide which parts of the terrace will be lit as early in the garden design process as possible, and before any flooring is laid, so that cables can be buried or at least hidden.

Unless you have experience in this field, you may prefer to work with a garden designer, if you have involved one, or with a lighting designer. You can find designers in all the major lighting showrooms or on exhibition stands at garden shows. They will, of course, recommend their own products, but will also provide useful information.

2. Choosing the lighting

Decide what sort of effect you want and then choose the ideal form of lighting to achieve it. Some of the many options are listed below. The quality of the fittings is crucial, as any inferior lights may corrode and stop working very quickly.

- *Uplighters will have to be as small as 8cm (3.5in) in depth and 5cm (2in) across if they are to be recessed into paving or decking. It is important to remember that they will get hot and should therefore not be used near areas where people will walk with bare feet. They are best used for "washing" a wall or skimming light across stones or steps.*

- *Downlighters can be fixed to the building or to the top of a feature such as a pergola or statue, from where they can direct light down to the floor.*

- *Path lights will indicate a route with a horizontal beam coming out of the side of a low domed fitting, thus preventing any annoying glare.*

- *Small spotlights on spikes made of copper or stainless steel can easily be installed in a bed to highlight a tree, focus on an ornament or illuminate a group of plants. Spotlights can be very effective, and they are a very popular form of garden lighting, but be aware that overuse can spoil the effect.*

above The plumes of the pampas grasses are transformed into an extraordinary decoration when illuminated, while indoor lighting, downlighters and candles create a golden pool of light against the night sky for an alfresco dinner.

- *Underwater lights in ponds or other water features create sensational effects — a night-time dip in the jacuzzi becomes a truly magical experience.*

- *Simple candles are still one of the most successful forms of ambient lighting. In a dining area, they work best in glass storm lanterns or large ornate copper lanterns. Elsewhere, they may be placed in galvanized lanterns on the floor for a restful and relaxing atmosphere.*

3. Installing the lighting

This is a complicated operation, and safety is crucial, so it is best left to the professionals. Some garden lighting operates on a low-voltage system, which is plugged into the house circuit via a transformer. Cabling for this can be laid on the ground, rather than needing to be buried, which makes the design more flexible. Other lighting may need mains voltage, and this involves heavily insulated cabling and waterproofed switch gear. The cables will need to be buried for safety, and so such systems should be installed before any flooring is laid to avoid any unnecessary disruption.

chapter four
sky-high gardening

With the hard landscaping and decorative
features now all in place, the time has finally
come to introduce the plants. As on the ground,
the plants for a roof terrace — ranging from
tall shrubs to tiny alpines — will perform
different functions: providing welcome shade
on a sunny day, creating a striking focal point,
adding a brilliant patch of colour, or providing
fresh fruit and vegetables for the table.
Balconies can also be transformed by plants in
pots, hanging baskets and troughs.

*left This brilliantly planted roof terrace seems to be totally unaffected by strong
winds, as the density of the planting and the use of screens have created a
protected micro-environment within London's Docklands.*

choosing the plants

The windswept top of a building may not offer the best growing conditions, but plants can still be grown here. Whether the design is minimal, with a few large structural plants, or is more like a country garden, with plants tumbling out of containers or climbing up structures, the plants must be robust.

below The clematis trained around one of the columns of this beautifully constructed pergola meets the equally immaculately pruned wisteria that runs over the top. Long, pale green beans follow the dangling purple flowers of the wisteria.

The choice of plant material for the roof terrace will be all-important, and obvious places to look to for inspiration are mountainous and seaside environments, which are equally battered by the wind and experience strong light. Any plants that can survive these conditions will feel at home on an exposed roof terrace.

Tough trees and shrubs acting as windbreaks will allow more delicate plants to flourish under their protection. These trees and shrubs may be planted singly or to form thick hedges. Others can then be added to bring structure and drama to the terrace. Such large specimens will be given centre-stage, and may form focal points.

Among these imposing trees and large shrubs there will be gaps that need to be filled. The best candidates for this are medium-sized shrubs such as rhododendrons and hydrangeas, as well as grasses, ferns and hostas. It is best to include some evergreens for year-round interest.

A traditional vegetable garden may seem an unlikely candidate for roof space, but there is no reason why salad leaves, tomatoes, herbs, and apples and pears should not be grown here, if suitably protected.

When buying plants and trees for the terrace, you should remember that they will probably have been grown in the relatively protected and monitored atmosphere of a nursery. Suddenly they will be transported, sometimes craned, to a rooftop, where they will most probably meet the full blast of the elements.

To make the transition as smooth as possible, prepare containers in advance, and fill with a suitable potting mix – preferably soil-based for most permanent plantings – laid on top of a layer of drainage material with a porous fabric in between.

above This roof garden demonstrates how a stark contemporary scheme in a very urban setting is in perfect harmony with the kind of soft perennial planting usually associated with traditional borders, with tall plants, such as Verbena bonariensis, at the back and creeping plants, such as silvery Stachys byzantina at the front.

right A stone pot filled with a mixture of silvery plants adds even more exuberance to the base of an arch already covered in climbing plants.

far right Herbs and vegetables can be grown in the most unlikely high places, as here within sight of the Empire State Building.

planting for shelter

Even if you are aware of the prevailing winds in your area, the configuration of neighbouring buildings or the way the terrace is built might create wind tunnels and unexpected turbulence. Whatever the wind direction, planting for shelter will make the terrace a calmer and more protected space.

From a design point of view, fixed screens might be a preferred choice to create shelter, but to give extra protection or to achieve a more natural look, a curtain of hardy evergreen plants able to withstand wind and cold is essential.

Conifers come top of the list of plants for shelter. Not only have they proved their hardiness on the slopes of mountains and exposed moorlands, but their colour and strong shapes are also great design assets. The Lawson's cypress (*Chamaecyparis lawsoniana*) and the bright green arbor vitae (*Thuja occidentalis*) have long been favourites as hedging and shelter belt plants, almost to the point of cliché. In the confined space of a roof terrace, however, they will be seen at closer range, and it will be possible to admire their intricate fronds and tiny cones as well as being grateful for their thick mantel.

If well managed, another conifer, the much-maligned Leyland cypress (*Cupressocyparis leylandii*), is also very useful. Its extremely rapid growth – 1.8m (6ft) three years after being planted as a cutting – has to be checked with a yearly clipping, but it will reward you with a tough, even hedge of a good green with no gaps or bare patches.

The paragon of hedging plants is undoubtedly the yew (*Taxus baccata*), which cannot be surpassed for colour and elegance or structural presence. It grows slowly and responds brilliantly to being sheared, and its smooth, velvety form will become a piece of living architecture.

Members of the eucalyptus group of hardy evergreens are too vigorous to be grown as trees. If bought as young plants, however, they respond very well to being regularly cut back and thus grown as multi-stemmed shrubs. In addition to being very tough and making a lovely rustling sound with their leaves in the wind, their aromatic, beautifully shaped, blue-grey leaves, delicate white flowers and interesting bark provide the instant sub-tropical effect often looked for by contemporary designers.

A holly (*Ilex*) is a noble addition to any planting scheme. It might not seem an obvious choice for a confined space, but numerous species are not prickly and, in addition to the variety of beautiful leaf colours from darkest green to striking variegations, female trees bear a profusion of bright red berries that last through the winter.

If what you need is a low screen, dense, evergreen shrubs such as box, *Viburnum tinus*, Japanese privet (*Ligustrum japonicum*) and Portuguese laurel (*Prunus lusitanica*) are all suitable choices for an exposed terrace.

opposite The many layers of planting on this mature terrace have created a most inviting, almost secret, garden, which will provide the perfect place to which to retreat in the heat of the summer.

top Two black pines protect the flowering perennials at their feet.

above A frothy dwarf conifer (Pinus mugo 'Mops') brings the right amount of softness to a black metal planter.

planting for accent

Now that the rooftop garden is sheltered and protected, it is time to choose the stars of the show: the trees and large shrubs that will form living sculptures and bring drama to the garden. They will be noticed for their shape, size, flowers or leaves, and be tough enough to withstand the harsh conditions.

adaptable trees

Trees look wonderful on a roof. Not only are they in proportion with the open space, but the fact that they are so far from their natural habitat also introduces a very thrilling, vertiginous feel to the garden.

Trees will greatly benefit from being grown in custom-made planters, since their size can be varied depending on the species chosen, thus allowing each tree to be displayed to its best advantage. When positioning the trees as focal points, make sure the weight is evenly distributed over the whole roof terrace.

Root pruning is essential to restrict the size of the trees: each year in autumn, the soil should be emptied out of the container and a quarter of the roots sawn off while they are still within the container, before fresh soil is added. This harsh-sounding measure, combined with a strict feeding regime, will keep trees in planters looking healthy and vigorous for years, and stop them outgrowing their containers.

Silver birches (*Betula pendula*) are great favourites for roof sites. Their gleaming white trunks are an asset all year around but particularly in winter, when they are resplendent against a dull sky. By contrast, a black pine (*Pinus austriaca*) cuts a stately silhouette against the sky and will thrive in the harsh rooftop conditions, as will the smaller mountain pine (*Pinus mugo*). Contrasting coloured planters will emphasize the drama of these trees.

Some of the dwarf conifers are also excellent choices as standard trees. They grow to a maximum of about 1.8m (6ft) and so are more manageable on a smaller terrace. The Japanese cedar (*Cryptomeria japonica*) is probably the most stunning of these dwarfs, with its neatly geometrical and velvety leaves of the most beautiful emerald green fitting perfectly against the muted grey of a galvanized planter.

A striking column effect can be achieved by planting a garden form of the juniper (either *Juniperus virginiana* 'Skyrocket' or *J. chinensis* 'Stricta') or the slender Italian cypress (*Cupressus sempervirens* 'Pyramidalis'). Their tops will bend in the wind. Wiring each tree in a spiral and clipping it regularly will help to retain its pencil-like shape.

opposite left This spectacular flowering crab apple (Malus), totally unaffected by both its position high in the New York sky and its relatively small planter, demonstrates the benefits of careful maintenance.

Evergreen magnolias (*Magnolia grandiflora*) hate to be blown about, but if a specimen is planted against a wall in a large Versailles case, it will look truly magnificent and will eventually reward you with huge, fragrant, white flowers.

Fruit trees would be a welcome, and novel, addition to a roof terrace. Training an apple tree (*Malus domestica*) or a pear tree (*Pyrus communis*) as an espalier against a wall or as a freestanding divider (cordon) would add a striking design element to any scheme. A crab apple, such as *Malus* 'Profusion', would be decorative with its mass of purple flowers and dark red fruit.

The palms, with their dramatic presence, should also be mentioned here. Only *Trachycarpus fortunei* is completely hardy, but in the artificially warmer microclimates of large cities, other palms, such as *Phoenix canariensis* or the lovely featherlike *Butia capitata*, could also be grown in a large Versailles case.

opposite below This olive tree (Olea europaea) gives a Mediterranean feel to a roof terrace. The silvery grey leaves add the finishing touch to a scheme of complementary tones.

below All these trees are happily growing in containers. From left to right: the extraordinary shape of a juniper (Juniperus) in a wooden planter; the white trunks of birch trees (Betula) *brightening up a winter's day in their galvanized planters; a black pine (Pinus austriaca) in a black metal pot; and a tall, mature pine tree echoing the adjacent tall service pipes.*

right The elegant galvanized spiral staircase seems to be leading right to the top of the tall pine tree, creating a wonderful element of surprise.

Some trees offer excellent autumn colours, and these will make wonderful additions to the garden just as the perennials and annuals have finished their displays, and the garden is in danger of looking a little bare.

The Japanese maples (*Acer palmatum*) have the most fantastic leaf colour, from ruby red to richest mahogany, with deeply cut leaves. They also have small reddish-purple flowers in spring. The names of the cultivars give you an idea of what to expect from these deciduous trees: 'Atropurpureum', 'Fireglow' and 'Garnet'. Some are green in spring but turn red, orange or yellow in autumn, such as 'Dissectum Atropurpureum'. Japanese maples are not the easiest plants to grow on a roof, as they hate cold winds and strong sunlight, but if you can give them some protection they are well worth trying, and can make the most beautiful focal points.

Amelanchier laevis, known in America as serviceberry and in Europe as snowy mespilus, is a small, delicately built, but tough tree that grows happily in a container. It also offers a succession of attractive features. A mass of long, pointed white buds first appear in spring, gradually opening against a backdrop of unfurling bronze leaves. The leaves then turn green to offset little dark berries before taking on the softest orange glow in autumn. To round off this list of assets. the *Amelanchier* responds very well to pruning.

Some of the dogwoods (*Cornus*) can also be grown here. The cornelian cherry (*Cornus mas*), which is resistant to exposure and dryness, is a good choice, as is the Japanese dogwood (*Cornus kousa*). Despite European gardeners' best efforts, however, the dogwoods never give the spectacular display they are famous for in North America. However, in Europe the gap could successfully be filled with *Cornus alba*, a shrub with wonderful red stems in winter, or *Cornus controversa* 'Variegata', a small tree with interestingly tiered growth and a cloud of tiny white flowers above the green and white leaves.

Large shrubs planted as specimens can equally attract the attention or frame a view. The smoke bush, green or red (*Cotinus coggygria* and *C. c.* 'Royal Purple'), with its haze of flowers in summer, the evergreen *Osmanthus*, or some of the many hebes would all be excellent choices. Other candidates include *Malvaviscus arboreus* – a vigorous evergreen that has bright red flowers in summer to autumn – and *Elaeagnus pungens* 'Maculata', a bushy evergeen with slightly spiny dark green leaves that have a central area of yellow; it has fragrant, urn-shaped, creamy white flowers in autumn

above left *With plenty of water hydrangeas grow very well in containers, and this H. quercifolia is particularly successful. Even though the white flowers have turned brown, they remain decorative against the oak-shaped leaves and will stay until the autumn, when they can be pruned back.*

above right *While magnolias are notorious wind-haters, this large evergreen M. grandiflora has thrived*

here in the shelter of the building to make a magnificent feature in a potentially difficult corner.

right *These olive trees (Olea europaea) look at home on this sheltered London terrace. The underplanting of lavender completes the Mediterranean atmosphere, making this spot the perfect place for a summer breakfast.*

planting as filler

For those with minimalist tastes, the accent plants may be sufficient planting for their rooftop garden to seem complete. For those who are passionate about plants, however, and want to create a softer, more profuse look, the gaps can be filled using some of the many suitable plants described here.

shrubs

opposite This terrace is so generously planted with a wonderful mixture of shrubs, bright perennials and annuals that the Empire State Building appears like a rather surreal backdrop to the bucolic scene.

below On this large New York terrace, the furthest area from the apartment has been given over to perennials to be admired in summer but not visible from inside in winter.

Fillers are the plants that introduce different heights, leaf forms and colours while creating a separate plane of vision. They help to give a feeling of being surrounded by nature. The choice is vast from among shrubs, perennials, annuals and grasses, and is constrained only by the hardiness and wind resistance of the plants.

The creeping junipers (*Juniperus horizontalis*), such as 'Prince of Wales' or 'Wiltonii', which are often overlooked, will hug containers and soften lines with excellent tones of green.

The large genus of the evergreen rhododendrons, natives of Bhutan and Myanmar (Burma), will be happy on a roof as long as they are grown in the right acid soil mix and are partially shaded so reproducing their native habitat. It might be best to choose from among the species rather than the hybrids, as the species are less dense and more elegant, often with brown underleaves. *Rhododendron aberconwayi* 'His Lordship' is white with crimson spots, *R. yakushimanum* has pale pink flowers and *R. cersimum* is a glorious crimson.

The viburnums are another excellent family to look to for a range of features and good nature. There is a variety for each season. *Viburnum* x *bodnantense* 'Dawn', a multi-stemmed shrub, will produce very fragrant pink flowers through most of the winter, cheering up any dull day, while the guelder rose (*V. opulus*) has lovely white flowers in early summer and shiny red berries against orange-red leaves in autumn. Finally, *V. tinus* has dark pink buds in early spring followed by white flowers.

Hydrangeas grow extremely well in containers, although they do need a lot of water. As a strong and elegant backdrop to other white flowers, such as the delicate gaura or the jewel-like *Astrantia major*, *Hydrangea paniculata* 'Grandiflora' and *H. quercifolia* have few rivals.

For scent, colour and the feel of summer, it is difficult to surpass lavender, with its grey leaves and purple flowers, both exuding fragrance. If it is not sufficiently hardy for the conditions, it can be replaced every year for continued pleasure. Otherwise, a severe pruning as soon as it has finished flowering will keep the plant healthy for many years. Rosemary gives a similar effect, with the added bonus that it can be used to flavour cooking on the barbecue.

right The recessed planters, well protected by the glass balustrade, allow for the successful growth of an array of perennials, from the purple of Verbena bonariensis to the delicate yellow of Achillea 'Moonshine'.

below This lively summer border illustrates how well annuals respond to the strong light of a roof garden, and what an explosion of colours can be provided by Helenium and Rudbeckia.

perennials, annuals and grasses

above The Hosta glauca is tumbling over its container, with all its beautiful leaves intact, a long way from preying slugs and snails. Surprisingly, the delicate-looking leaves are very resistant to the wind.

Should you wish for a green garden, hostas and ferns will be your first choice. Hostas are particularly satisfying to grow on a rooftop, as their lush leaves, so far away from any slugs and snails, remain pristine. There is a wide range of leaf colours, and many are variegated: *Hosta fortunei* 'Albopicta' has creamy-yellow leaves with dark green edges, while *H.* 'Halcyon' is a soft blue-grey. Though grown mainly for their leaves, hostas also bear delicate spikes of white or pale purple flowers in summer. Hardy ferns such as *Polypodium vulgare* and *Athyrium felix-femina*, like hostas, are happy in shade, and the unfurling of their new fronds in spring has a magical quality. For a sunnier spot, tall, deep blue agapanthus are great in containers, flowering better each year as they become more congested. They may need protection in winter, though.

Another very successful perennial on a roof is the daylily (*Hemerocallis*). Not only are the grass-like leaves very decorative and persistent, but the flowers, which last only a day, are produced in succession for 6–8 weeks. The colour range is impressive, from palest cream and golden yellow to deepest bronze and almost black, and some of the flowers are very fragrant.

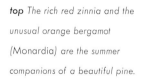

top The rich red zinnia and the unusual orange bergamot (Monardia) are the summer companions of a beautiful pine.

above The palm Phoenix canariensis has been placed in front of a thin metal trellis and is reflected in the coppery sphere.

above right Grasses use the slightest breeze to display their full glory, shimmering and undulating like this wonderful mature Pennisetum villosum in full bloom.

To create a scheme of hot colours, which is certainly the best choice in strong light, they could be combined with big sweeps of annuals such as the particularly lovely small *Rudbeckia triloba* or a *Helenium* in deep amber or dark orange. Other annuals, such as pelargoniums, cosmos, lobelia, busy Lizzies (*Impatiens*), and *Nigella*, can be used to fill any gaps.

The undisputed stars up on the roof are undoubtedly the grasses. They seem to be made for these conditions, rustling in the slightest breeze and shimmering in the faintest ray of sunshine. The most statuesque is the pampas grass (*Cortaderia selloana*), which is evergreen and produces dramatic, silvery white, feathery plumes in summer. Grown in a row of large planters, they would create a perfect backdrop to a lounging area.

Less dominant grasses, such as *Stipa* or *Miscanthus*, will mix with other plants to create pools of green among hotter colours, while the bright red *Imperata cylindrica* 'Rubra' could be used in contrast with dark blue *Iris sibirica*. Finally, planted in a large group, the ground-hugging *Ophiopogon planiscapus* 'Nigrescens' could give the illusion of an almost black "lawn".

left and below left This extraordinary vegetable garden is situated on top of a town house in Manhattan belonging to the Earth Pledge Foundation. As part of their "Green Roof Initiative", it aims to exploit unused space while improving insulation of buildings. Plants are grown in varying depths of expanded slate and fed once a month with a fish-waste product that is alive with enzymes. This crop of beautiful aubergines (eggplants) (Solanum melongena) is proof that the experiment is working.

below right Even on a windy rooftop it is possible to grow delicate peaches, as long as they are protected, as here by a simple fence of vertical posts.

planting for food

Planting a kitchen garden up at roof level is an exciting challenge and not so impossible as might first appear. The conditions are perfect for most of the herbs, and vegetables too will benefit from strong light, if they have some protection from the wind. Even some fruit can be grown successfully.

There are two ways to approach kitchen gardening on the roof: it can be a permanent part of the overall design or it can be a seasonal and temporary affair to be renewed or not, depending on enthusiasm and free time. The difference is that the same crops are simply grown in different containers.

As an integral part of the design, the vegetable garden could be arranged according to a traditional cruciform plan with a central feature. This could be a fountain or perhaps a dining table and chairs, to stress that the fresh produce grown in the custom-made beds will soon be enjoyed at the table. These beds could be made of reclaimed timber and faced with woven willow panels, making them decorative as well as easy to work in. Large galvanized planters will create a similar effect but in a more contemporary idiom.

Courgettes (zucchini) (*Cucurbita pepo*) can be used to cover the ground spectacularly, with the added bonus of their rich yellow flowers. Tomatoes (*Lycopersicon esculentum*) trained on vertical posts are very decorative, as are runner (green) beans (*Phaseolus coccinus*), with their vivid red flowers. If potatoes (*Solanum tuberosum*) are added to the list, the vegetable garden will provide many summer meals.

Apple (*Malus domestica*) or pear (*Pyrus communis*) trees trained as cordons to edge the planters will mark out the garden as well as producing lovely blossom in spring and delicious fruit in summer.

Growing herbs is a good way to start a vegetable garden, since they are easy and their profuse growth gives an instant feel of abundance. Thyme (*Thymus*) will tumble over the side of the planters, the scent of rosemary (*Rosmarinus*) will get stronger in the sunshine, and chives (*Allium schoenoprasum*) will make an excellent edging plant. Finally, a bay tree (*Laurus nobilis*) could be planted as a striking centrepiece.

To keep to the spirit of a vegetable garden and also to add decoration, it is perfectly in keeping to intersperse the vegetables and herbs with flowers, such as bright orange marigolds (*Calendula*) or brilliantly white marguerites (*Chrysanthemum frutescens*).

If, however, growing a few vegetables and herbs is only a temporary occupation, then single pots or growing bags can be used to form an ever-changing display throughout the summer. Growing bags do have the problem of being rather unsightly, in their often brightly coloured plastic, but they could be hidden behind other pots. Alternatively, a raised bed of black plastic is more easily camouflaged and can be stored flat in winter.

above Even in the most urban of situations, edible plants and flowers can successfully thrive, and look wonderful as well as producing delicious crops.

planting for balconies

Balconies are ideal for displaying plants, especially if they have open railings, so that the tumbling flowers can be seen by both the owners and passers-by. The choice of suitable flowers for troughs and baskets is limited only by the conditions offered by the balcony: sunny or shady.

above This balcony in Seville shows the planting at its most traditional and successful. This is the kingdom of ivy-leaved geraniums in tones of pink and red tumbling from every possible container in miraculous cascades.

right A series of balconies works best when all the owners are passionate gardeners and the various schemes appear to create cascades of flowering plants down the front of the building.

The starting point for balcony displays is the installation of long, shallow troughs fixed to the railings of an open balcony or to the top of the parapet wall. These immediately create a first plane of vision and define the space. Troughs can be bought off-the-shelf in suitable lengths made of galvanized metal, painted timber with a waterproof liner or black plastic, which is light and inexpensive and will soon disappear under a mass of flowers.

Hanging baskets are also an option. Suspended from the floor of the balcony above, or from a brise-soleil, these baskets will provide a welcome splash of colour at eye level. Another way of providing colour at this height is to attach wall planters to the front of the building, or, if they are made of brick or concrete, to the dividers or the parapet wall.

A favourite balcony plant is the trailing red geranium, such as *Pelargonium* 'Yale', which tumbles down in incredible profusion throughout the summer. As an alternative, or an accompaniment, to bright red geraniums, there are white varieties such as *P.* 'Mauritania' or pale pinks such as the double *P.* 'Butterfly Lorelei'. They will tolerate some neglect and drought, but regular deadheading, feeding and watering will ensure they give the best possible performance. A good companion for geraniums is a finely cut dark green ivy, such as *Hedera helix* 'Pedata', which will still be thriving in winter.

Another easy plant is the petunia, with colourful flowers from deepest purple to pale blue and dark red; the Surfinia varieties such as 'Blue Vein' are the best for trailing. *Verbena* x *hybrida* in purple to bright red will tumble over the container all through the season, while the highly attractive *Diascia* will flower throughout the summer into late autumn. Choose from named hybrids such as 'Pink Queen' and 'Lilac Belle'.

Fuchsias can make a splendid impact: bush varieties will give height to the display, while cascading varieties will drip their flowers through the balcony railings or from hanging baskets all through the summer. These are spectacular used to make up a trough or basket on their own, or they could be teamed with alyssum (*Lobularia maritima*) for contrast.

For a shady balcony, a mixture of tuberous begonias and busy Lizzies, both available in many colours, would be successful, and the well-loved lobelia (*Lobelia erinus*), in varieties such as 'Blue Cascade' or 'Cambridge Blue', will fill every available space in a wonderful cascading mass.

For spring, any combination of dwarf bulbs – daffodils such as *Narcissus* 'Bantam', and tulips such as *Tulipa kauf-manniana* – combined with violas or primulas, would make a cheerful display to mark the end of winter.

If there is room, large pots can be positioned on the balcony for planting larger specimens or climbers, as they would be on a roof terrace. Rows of smaller pots could be used for floor-level displays of perennials, annuals or bulbs; alternatively, they could contain a variety of herbs and salad leaves for summer dining.

above When all the containers disappear under a mass of plants, even on a small balcony the illusion of a garden can be recreated, particularly if, as here, the landscape beyond offers the perfect backdrop.

left It seems impossible to believe that a balcony hides behind this exuberant planting of Ipomoea, Clematis tangutica and Helichrysum, among other plants.

case study: *secluded planting*

When sitting out on this terrace in one of the elegant chairs, it is difficult to imagine that you are on a roof high up in the New York sky. This large "wrap-around" space contains a luxuriant garden, full of plants that change with the seasons, as well as some stately evergreens to give it structure.

left *This is the first point of entry to the terrace, invitingly set under a large awning and the perfect transition from the inside space.*

below *The planting is well established and very successful, as shown here by this mass of white roses, which create a division.*

opposite bottom left *The low wooden troughs on top of the parapet walls are planted with a mixture of conifers and annuals that do not interrupt the view.*

opposite bottom right *Continuing the walk around, the terrace opens up into another area, set for relaxing with beautiful loungers among a dazzling array of thriving plants.*

The large size of this impressive terrace meant that there was plenty of scope for the designer to create a garden that was full of interest and variety. The area has been divided into a succession of smaller spaces, each secluded by planting and completely self-contained. The large scale of this terrace has, however, meant that only part of its plan can be shown overleaf.

From the reception room, sliding doors lead on to a narrow part of the terrace that is completely covered over by an awning. Underneath, a low table and chairs are invitingly arranged for a morning coffee or an evening drink. A row of low timber planters on top of the parapet wall, which are brimming over with trailing plants and colourful annuals, does not obstruct the stunning view of the Reservoir in Central Park when you are standing, but reinforces the feeling of intimacy for those seated in the chairs.

As you move around the terrace, you discover several different areas among rows of tall trees and shrubs against the walls of the apartment, such as birch (*Betula*), magnolia, beech (*Fagus*) and *Cotinus* underplanted with a mixture of annuals, such as *Bacopa* or *Cleum*. One area has low tables and chairs and a few loungers, and planters filled with the same combination of trailing plants and colourful annuals are placed on the parapet wall. Some areas are divided by timber planters at right angles from the building; these overflow with white roses or creeping conifers. Still other areas are enclosed by majestic pine trees (*Pinus*) and festooned with grasses (*Pennisetum villosum*) or edged with spirea balls underplanted with bright blue petunias and silver *Helichrysum* for summer.

The final area you come to, past a herb garden, is a raised timber deck with a large dining table that is easily reached from the kitchen of the apartment. Containers planted with hydrangeas and *Pittosporum* are placed so as not to interrupt the view from the table.

Unity is given to the whole space by the very ingenious use of a flooring material you would not expect here: perforated black rubber tiles usually found in swimming pools, which are cheap and easy to install as well as extremely durable. The furniture is another unifying element. Beautifully shaped in metal mesh, with pale grey cushions, it adds a very contemporary note to this otherwise traditional and extremely well-thought-out roof garden.

below A second set of table and chairs has been placed invitingly at the end of a densely planted alley. The planting has been kept low by the parapet so that the view of the city is uninterrupted.

left The dining area is slightly raised and revealed at the very end of the terrace, where it can be entered from the kitchen. A yellow pine deck is laid in a basket-weave pattern.

below Trees have been planted along the whole length of the building and have fared extremely well, as this eccentric birch, spruce and *Magnolia grandiflora* all demonstrate.

Due to the large scale of this terrace, only part of the plan is reproduced here. It shows the herb garden and the raised deck with dining area.

left Looking towards the dining area, the mass of the planting is clearly seen. The taller plants are kept against the building to leave the city in full view, including a splendid water tower so evocative of the New York skyline.

right Black perforated rubber tiles are used on this section and the remaining (unshown) sections of the terrace as an ingenious way to cover an uneven surface and unify the space.

Building a timber planter

With the extraordinary choice of planters now available, many of them highly decorative in their own right, it might seem unnecessary to build your own. However, if you want a really lush display of plants on a roof terrace, a custom-made planter, which can provide the maximum possible volume of soil for the available space, will probably be the best option.

1. Choosing the site

The edge of the terrace will most probably be recommended as the best site for positioning planters, though some areas may have to be reinforced if the planters are large. Check with a structural engineer before starting work. Smaller planter boxes, up to 50cm (20in) deep, will be easier to position.

2. Choosing the materials

The best way to build a planter is to choose a box made of galvanized metal or plastic, as these materials will be completely waterproof and in no danger of rotting, and then clad it with timber. Alternatively, light fibreglass containers can be made to measure and are probably the best material to use on a roof.

It might be tempting just to line a wooden box with strong plastic sheeting or to paint it with a waterproofing product, but this is never a long-term solution, as the wood will eventually come into contact with the wet soil.

The cladding is a matter of taste. Rough pine, cut into planks 15cm (6in) wide and 5cm (2in) thick and left natural, can be used throughout. Alternatively, thinner pine planks could be used, and they could be painted or stained.

Cedar is another good choice, as it is light. Finally, green oak will be easy to work with and is easy to source in most countries.

3. Assembling the planter

There are many different ways of cladding the planter. The four planks that make up each tier could be overlapped in alternate directions, creating an interesting pattern of plank ends and faces and giving strength to the box (see left). Another method would be to overlap (shiplap) the slats and fix them to a bottom and top band.

A third choice would be to use different widths of timber, along the lines on which the traditional Versailles case is built: for example, 8 x 8cm (3 x 3in) for the corners, 6 x 6cm (2.5 x 2.5in) for the top bands and 10 x 10cm (4 x 4in) for the upright slats. This might be a more difficult method of construction, but it will produce an elegant planter. A carpenter could be commissioned to make such planters.

Any of these designs can be used on any size of terrace, whether you build:
- a single planter for a specimen plant (as used on this terrace for a Siberian spruce (Picea obovata) see below),
- a series of planters to create a narrow (20cm/8in) border (as used here for a herb garden), or
- some shallow (20cm/8in) planters to sit on top of a parapet wall (as used here with trailing plants and colourful annuals).

chapter five

plant directory

It is impossible to think of a garden without

plants, and a garden in the sky is no exception.

It will, however, demand container plants, and

although with good care any plant can be

grown in a container, such an exposed location

does create very particular demands. This

directory focuses on plants that have been

chosen for their ability to do well on a windy

roof as well as adding to any chosen design

with colour, shape or scent.

left *This group of Crocosmia is an excellent choice for the roof garden as the vibrant red glows in the strong light while the stiff stems and long thin leaves cope perfectly with the wind.*

trees and shrubs

Trees and shrubs provide the essential framework of your roof terrace. The species suggested here are reliable growers and many will withstand extreme conditions. They also offer a range of interesting features, from beautiful bark to striking flowers and stunning outline.

Amelanchier laevis
Serviceberry, snowy mespilus
This graceful, deciduous, spreading tree has a profusion of delicate white flowers in spring opening against coppery young leaves. The leaves turn green in summer as a foil to fleshy black berries, and then produce a splendid display of scarlet and orange in autumn.
Height and spread: to 4m (13ft) in a container.
Hardiness: Fully hardy 5–7.
Cultivation: Grow in lime-free, soil-based potting mix in sun or semi-shade.

Betula utilis
Himalayan birch
This deciduous tree is grown mainly for its silky, paper-thin, peeling white bark and its hardiness. Long brown catkins appear in autumn, creating extra winter interest until they expand in spring. The leaves are dark above and paler underneath. *Betula pendula* (silver birch, Zones 3–8) is another excellent variety.
Height: 4m (13ft).

Amelanchier laevis

Spread: 1.5m (5ft).
Hardiness: Fully hardy 6–8.
Cultivation: Grow in fertile, well-drained but moist potting mix, in a sunny position. Prune regularly.

Buddleja davidii 'Black Knight'
Butterfly bush
The dark green leaves of this deciduous, resilient shrub are long and pointed with a felty white underside. The flowers, which are deepest dark purple, are very fragrant and will attract butterflies to your roof garden throughout the summer months. 'Royal Red' has rich red flowers, and 'Harlequin' has purple flowers and attractively variegated leaves with creamy white markings. B. 'Lochinch' has fragrant, lilac-blue flowers above grey-green leaves.
Height and spread: 3m (10ft).
Hardiness: Fully hardy 5–9.
Cultivation: Grow in fertile, well-drained soil in full sun. Prune hard (down to 15cm/6in from the soil level) in early spring to keep the overall shape of the graceful, arching branches.

Buxus sempervirens

Cercis siliquastrum

Buxus sempervirens
Box
This evergreen shrub of excellent foliage and habit responds very well to clipping and is used extensively for hedging, edging and topiary work. It has oblong, glossy, dark green leaves and will create an excellent screen up to 1.5m (5ft) high. The variety B. s. 'Suffruticosa' (bushy and slow-growing with a tight mass of bright green leaves) is perfect grown as a low border to define the edge of a planter.
Height: 15cm–1.5m (6in–5ft).
Spread: 15cm–1m (6in–3ft).
Hardiness: Fully hardy 6–9.
Cultivation: Grow in soil-based potting mix with extra grit for drainage, in any aspect. Prune in midsummer. If drastic cutting back is needed to keep the plant healthy, it will always re-grow from the wood.

Cercis siliquastrum
Judas tree, redbud
Beautiful, heart-shaped, waxy green leaves and a dense mass of pea-like rosy flowers are the reasons for growing this deciduous bushy tree. The flowers are followed by long, purplish seed pods, which may remain on the tree throughout winter. The leaves turn yellow in autumn before falling.
Height and spread: 4m (13ft).
Hardiness: Fully hardy 8–9.
Cultivation: Grow in deep, fertile, well-drained soil mix in full sun.

Cordyline australis
Cabbage tree
This evergreen tree of very striking outline has a solid trunk or sometimes several topped by a crown of long, arching, green leaves. It has small, scented white flowers in large panicles in early summer, and white fruit in autumn. The variety 'Atropurpurea' has dark red leaves and is slightly less hardy than the green type.
Height: 4m (13ft).
Spread: 2m (6ft).
Hardiness: Half hardy 10.
Cultivation: Grow in fertile, well-drained soil in full light or partial shade. Remove dying leaves at the bottom of the crown.

Crataegus prunifolia

Crataegus prunifolia
Hawthorn
The shiny, dark green, oval leaves of this deciduous tree turn red and orange in autumn. It produces a mass of white flowers with pink centres in spring, followed by dark red fruit. It is extremely tough – unaffected by wind or pollution – and so perfect for an exposed site.
Height and spread: 5m (16ft).
Hardiness: Fully hardy 6–7.
Cultivation: Grow in fertile, well-drained soil mix, preferably in sun, though it is tolerant of most conditions. It can be grown in exposed positions. Prune regularly.

Eucalyptus niphophila
Snow gum, alpine snow gum
For use in containers, this vigorous evergreen tree is best grown as a shrub by cutting it back regularly to 30cm (12in) from the ground. The blue-grey leaves with their red edging release a fragrant oil when touched. The flowers are white with many stamens. The white and grey bark peels in extremely attractive patterns.
Height: 4m (13ft).
Spread: 1m (3ft).
Hardiness: Fully hardy 8–10.
Cultivation: Grow in fertile, well-drained soil mix in sun.

Fuchsia magellanica
Lady's eardrops
This deciduous shrub is grown for its pendulous bicoloured flowers of purple petals, long red tubes and sepals, which are followed by black fruits. F. 'Tom Thumb' (Zones 8–10) is a very free-flowering dwarf form with mauve-purple petals.
Height and spread: 50cm–2m (20in–6ft).
Hardiness: Frost hardy.
Cultivation: Grow in fertile, well-drained soil in a partially sheltered and shaded position. If the top growth dies in winter, cut it back in spring.

Hebe salicifolia
An evergreen upright shrub, this has long, narrow, pale green leaves and very long-lasting spikes of white or pale lilac-blue flowers. It is very useful with other planting but is equally good on its own, as it always emerges pristine after a rainstorm or a snowfall.
Height and spread: 1m (3ft).
Hardiness: Fully hardy 9–10.
Cultivation: Grow in well-drained soil mix in full sun. Cut back in spring if it gets leggy.

Hibiscus syriacus
Dark green leaves and beautiful, large, trumpet-shaped flowers make this deciduous shrub very distinctive. A large number of cultivars have been developed from this upright deciduous species: 'Blue Bird' (lilac-blue flowers with a red centre), 'Red Heart' (white flowers with a very conspicuous red centre) and 'Diana' (very large pure white flowers) are all in flower from late summer to mid-autumn.
Height and spread: 2m (6ft).
Hardiness: Fully hardy 6–9.
Cultivation: Grow in humus-rich, well-drained soil in full sun.

Hydrangea
These deciduous shrubs with showy flowers are a perfect choice for growing in containers on a roof. H. macrophylla 'Madame E. Mouillère' (Zones 6–9) is a rounded shrub in the Hortensia group, with dark green leaves. The large white florets have pink or blue eyes. H. paniculata 'Grandiflora' (Zones 4–8) has long, oval, dark green leaves and conical white flowers, later turning deep pink. H. quercifolia (Zones 5–9) is a bushy shrub with conical white flowers; its beautifully cut leaves have magnificent bronze tints in autumn.
Height and spread: to 2m (6ft).
Hardiness: Fully hardy.

Cultivation: Grow in humus-rich, moist, well-drained soil. Keep well watered in the dry season. Cut back H. macrophylla immediately after flowering, and prune H. paniculata hard back in spring.

Ilex
Holly
Its shiny leaves and fruit of varying colours produced on female plants make this beautiful evergreen shrub a wonderful addition to any scheme. The species recommended here have non-spiky leaves. I. crenata

Eucalyptus niphophila

(Zones 6–8) is a compact shrub with small, oval, dark green leaves, bearing glossy black fruit in autumn. I. aquifolium 'J.C. Van Tol' (Zones 7–9) has dark purple young branches and red berries. Its dark green leaves are slightly spiny. The leaves of its sport, 'Golden Van Tol', have yellow edges. I. 'Nellie R. Stevens' (Zones 6–8) is free-fruiting.
Height: 3m (10ft).
Spread: 1.5m (5ft).
Hardiness: Fully to frost hardy.
Cultivation: Grow in fertile, well-drained soil in sun or semi-shade.

Hydrangea quercifolia 'Snow Flake'

Hibiscus syriacus 'Diana'

Juniperus
Juniper
The pencil form of *J. virginiana*, with its grey-green aromatic needles and fleshy dark berries, makes it a striking accent plant either acting as a sentinel at the entrance to the garden or marking the end of a vista. *J. horizontalis* 'Wiltonii' is a creeping form of the evergreen conifer with bluish-grey leaves, perfect for a large container or a long, low planter.
Height: 50cm–5m (20in–16ft).
Spread: 1–1.5m (3–5ft).
Hardiness: Fully hardy 3–9.
Cultivation: Grow in ericaceous (acid) soil in full sun.

Laurus
Use this evergreen shrub, with its mid-green, large, glossy leaves, to create a very lush divider within the terrace. *L. nobilis*, the bay tree, is one of the easiest plants on which to try your skills at topiary, and its leaves can be used in cooking.
Height: to 4m (13ft).
Spread: 2m (6ft).
Hardiness: Frost hardy 8–10.
Cultivation: Grow in fertile, well-drained soil in sun or semi-shade with some protection.

Lavandula angustifolia
Lavender
Its scented, grey-green leaves and very fragrant purple flowers make this evergreen shrub a must on a roof. The best varieties are 'Hidcote' (deep lavender-blue flowers) and 'Munstead' (lilac-blue flowers), both with long, narrow leaves, of which the latter is more compact. When in bloom lavender is irresistible to bees, which can be a problem.
Height and spread: 60cm–1m (2–3ft).
Hardiness: Fully hardy 6–9.
Cultivation: Grow in very well-drained soil in full sun. To keep the shape of the shrubs, whether grown singly or as a low hedge, prune them hard immediately after flowering, and then again lightly in spring if necessary.

Ligustrum
Privet
This dense, evergreen shrub, highly valued for its toughness, is often used for hedging but responds very well to being clipped into shapes such as balls and spirals. *L. japonicum* has bigger, glossy leaves and large panicles of fragrant white flowers in the summer.
Height: 3m (10ft).
Spread: 1.5m (5ft).
Hardiness: Fully hardy 7–9.
Cultivation: Grow in well-drained soil in most aspects.

Magnolia grandiflora
Bull bay, laurel magnolia
A mature specimen of this conical evergreen tree will bear large, fragrant, creamy white flowers in spring, making a spectacular display. Its oval, glossy, mid-green leaves have a rusty underside. Magnolias hate wind, so you should consider growing one only if it can be sheltered by a wall or a tall screen. Ideally, they should be planted against a sunny wall.
Height: 4m (13ft).
Spread: 2.5m (8ft).
Hardiness: Frost hardy 7–9.
Cultivation: Grow in humus-rich, ericaceous (acid), well-drained soil in sun or semi-shade.

Malus
Crab apple
An abundance of cup-shaped flowers, small, long-lasting fruit and good autumn colour make this deciduous tree very decorative, and the perfect way of introducing colour and fruit to a garden. 'John Downie' is one of the finest crab apples and has white flowers and orange-red fruit, which can be used to make jelly. It has narrow upright growth to start with, then changes to a more conical shape as it ages. *M. prunifolia* has lovely shaped leaves, fragrant white flowers and red fruit.
Height and spread: 4m (13ft).
Hardiness: Fully hardy 5–8.
Cultivation: Grow in fertile, well-drained soil, preferably in full sun.

Malus domestica
Apple tree
Edible fruit follows a cloud of pale pink blossom on this deciduous tree. Apple trees can be successfully trained against a wall into an espalier, which will be both decorative and space saving, or into a cordon to form a low division. It is best to get the advice of a reliable nursery to choose the best variety for your area and conditions. 'Garden Sun Red' produces large red and yellow apples.
Height: to 5m (16ft).
Spread: to 4m (13ft).
Hardiness: Fully hardy 5–8.
Cultivation: Grow in fertile soil in full sun.

Pinus nigra
Black pine
This evergreen conifer, which is very tolerant of wind and exposure, grows into a tree of interesting shape with long needles of a very good green. It also produces cones, though these are small during its first year, and take two years to ripen. It acts as a very effective windbreak and creates a focal point of great character for the roof-terrace garden.
Height: 5m (16ft).
Spread: 2.5m (8ft).
Hardiness: Fully hardy 5–8.
Cultivation: Grow in light, rich, well-drained soil in full sun. Root-prune to control its growth.

Pittosporum tobira
This bushy, evergreen shrub has dark green, glossy leaves and very fragrant, star-shaped, white flowers in late spring that later turn creamy yellow. Several plants could be grown in a row to create a pleasant low scented hedge near a sitting area; alternatively one could be grown singly in a large terracotta pot.
Height and spread: 1.5m (5ft).
Hardiness: Half hardy 8–10.
Cultivation: Grow in fertile, well-drained soil in sun or partial shade. Prune lightly in spring, if necessary, to keep its lovely rounded shape.

Laurus nobilis

Ligustrum

Malus 'John Downie'

Pittosporum tobira 'Wheeler's Dwarf'

Prunus lusitanica
Portuguese laurel
Lovely glossy, dark green leaves and red stems make this a very useful evergreen shrub. Pruned hard in spring, it will form an excellent hedge or an interesting centrepiece. It bears small white fragrant flowers in summer followed by oval deep purple fruit.
Height and spread: to 3m (10ft).
Hardiness: Frost hardy 7–9.
Cultivation: Grow in any well-drained soil in sun or shade.

Pyrus communis
Pear
This deciduous tree produces edible fruit after a haze of wonderful white blossom. Pear trees can be trained as espaliers against a wall or as cordons to form a low division. As for apple trees, it is best to seek advice from a reliable nursery to choose the best variety for your climate and growing conditions. 'Angelina' is a prolific producer of large yellow and vermilion pears.
Height: to 5m (16ft).
Spread: to 4m (13ft).
Hardiness: Fully hardy 5–9.
Cultivation: Grow in fertile, well-drained soil in full sun.

Rosmarinus officinalis
Rosemary
The aromatic leaves of this evergreen shrub can be used in cooking. Small, purple-blue flowers appear in spring to early summer. It can be grown in a single pot or planted as a low, fragrant hedge. 'Prostratus' is a creeping form, slightly less hardy than other varieties. 'Miss Jessop's Upright' is good for hedging. It has small blue flowers from mid- to late spring and occasionally also in autumn.
Height and spread: to 1m (3ft).
Hardiness: Frost hardy 7–9.
Cultivation: Grow in free-draining, light soil in full sun. Prune hedges hard immediately after flowering and again lightly in spring, if necessary, to stop the plants from becoming leggy.

Salvia
Sage
This group includes mainly evergreen shrubs with long, slender, tubular flowers with two lips. S. fulgens (Zones 9–10) is a tall evergreen with whirls of bright red flowers. S. officinalis 'Purpurascens' (Zones 6–9), which is a bushy evergreen shrub with aromatic grey-purple young leaves and blue flowers, introduces a good contrast in colour among the greens.
Height and spread: 60cm–1m (2–3ft).
Hardiness: Fully to half hardy.
Cultivation: Grow in well-drained soil in full sun.

Taxus baccata
Yew
This slow-growing dark green conifer, with its dense, velvety growth, is probably the best of all the hedging plants. It can be cut back hard to keep its shape. The flattened, needle-like leaves are dark green. Small, cup-shaped red fruits appear in autumn on female plants. Two variegated varieties are 'Dovastonii Aurea' (golden shoots and yellow-edged leaves) and 'Fastigiata Aurea' (with gold-variegated leaves).
Height and spread: to 2m (6ft) in a container.
Hardiness: Fully hardy 6–7.
Cultivation: Grow in good free-draining soil in sun or partial shade.

Trachycarpus
Chusan palm, windmill palm
This evergreen palm has huge bunches of tiny yellow flowers in summer and large glossy leaves. T. fortunei (Windmill palm) has a spectacular head of large, deeply divided, fan-like leaves, and has sprays of fragrant yellow flowers in early summer.
Height: to 5m (16ft).
Spread: to 3m (10ft).
Hardiness: Frost hardy 8–10.
Cultivation: Grow in fertile, well-drained soil, in a sheltered, sunny position. In winter protect young plants with horticultural fleece.

Viburnum
This very versatile group of deciduous and evergreen shrubs has many valuable uses. Some are grown for their flowers (winter or spring), others for their berries. V. x bodnantense 'Dawn' (Zones 7–9) is perfect in winter. It is deciduous and produces very fragrant, tubular, pinkish white flowers in winter and early spring. V. opulus (Zones 4–8) is deciduous, with lovely lace-cap white flowers in spring, dark green leaves turning red in autumn, and fruits that look very much like redcurrants. V. tinus 'Eve Price' (Zones 7–9) is evergreen with dark pink buds in winter and spring, followed by star-shaped white flowers and oval blue fruit.
Height and spread: to 3m (10ft).
Hardiness: Fully hardy.
Cultivation: Grow in fertile, well-drained soil in sun or partial shade.

Rosmarinus officinalis

Salvia officinalis 'Purpurascens'

Trachycarpus fortunei

climbers

This group of plants plays an important part on a roof terrace by adorning boundaries or vertical structures. Most climbers are vigorous and will require large containers and regular feeding, but they will reward you with a range of flowers and leaf shapes that provide interest all year round.

Campsis radicans

Clematis 'Jackmanii'

Campsis radicans
Trumpet vine, trumpet creeper
The woody stems of this very vigorous deciduous climber are covered with deeply cut leaves and clusters of very showy orange-red trumpet flowers in summer and early autumn.
Height and spread: to 10m (33ft).
Hardiness: Frost hardy 5–9.
Cultivation: Grow in fertile soil in full sun. Prune in spring to keep its prolific growth in check.

Clematis
With so many varieties available, clematis can provide interest almost all year round. *C. armandii* (Zones 7–9) is evergreen and vigorous, with scented white flowers in late winter. *C.* 'Jackmanii' (Zones 3–9) has large, deep purple flowers in summer. *C. viticella* (Zones 5–9) is late-flowering; 'Etoile Violette' has small, nodding, purple flowers, 'Pagoda' has deep pink flowers.
Height and spread: 3–10m (10–33ft).
Hardiness: Fully to half hardy.
Cultivation: Grow in fertile soil in sun or partial shade, keeping the roots in shade. The various species are divided into Groups 1, 2 and 3, and have different pruning requirements: refer to a specialist guide for details.

Cobaea scandens
Cup-and-saucer vine
This is a very interesting and useful climber that is grown as an annual and does not mind the shade. It has strong stems armed with tendrils that can quickly cover an arch or a pergola, where you can admire its extraordinary bell-shaped flowers with frilly collars, opening lime-green and turning purple as they age.

Height and spread: 4–5m (13–16ft).
Hardiness: Frost tender 9–10.
Cultivation: Grow in fertile soil in partial shade.

Hedera
Ivy
Plants of this evergreen, woody-stemmed, self-clinging perennial, either climbing or trailing, are very useful for introducing a pool of green with a great variety of leaf shapes in the most inhospitable conditions. *H. algeriensis* (Zones 9–10) has triangular leaves with purplish stems. *H. helix* 'Pedata' (Zones 5–9) has beautiful cruciform leaves. *H. hibernica* (Zones 5–9) is extremely tough and fast-growing, with good, mid-green leaves.
Height and spread: to 10m (33ft).
Hardiness: Frost to fully hardy.
Cultivation: Grow in any soil, in any aspect, although large-leaved forms do better in sun. To avoid a "nest" effect against a wall, cut the plant right back to the main frame in winter. It will look alarmingly bare at first but will grow back very quickly.

Hedera helix 'Pedata'

Hydrangea petiolaris
Climbing hydrangea

This deciduous woody, self-clinging climber has creamy white lace-cap flowers in summer. Usually after two years the plant will establish itself and begin to grow quickly, covering a wall or fence beautifully, even in full shade.

Height and spread: to 10m (33ft).
Hardiness: Fully hardy 4–9.
Cultivation: Grow in fertile, well-drained soil. Young plants should be stapled to the wall, fence or other support to encourage climbing while they establish themselves.

Ipomoea purpurea
Morning glory

As its name suggests, the trumpet-shaped flowers of this twining climber, with a white throat, open in the morning sun and close in the afternoon. Despite being a perennial, Ipomoea is usually grown as an annual, and although it is not always successful, it is well worth attempting for a Mediterranean feel to the garden during summer and early autumn. The stems are soft and hairy, and the leaves, which are sparingly borne, are heart-shaped.

Height and spread: to 5m (16ft).
Hardiness: Frost tender 10.
Cultivation: Grow in any fertile soil in full sun.

Jasminum officinale
Common white jasmine

This semi-evergreen climber has slender, twining, woody stems and headily fragrant flowers, from midsummer to autumn, that are white inside and pink outside. It can be happily grown against a warm wall or over a pergola, where its strong, heady scent is sure to conjure up the pleasures of a summer evening.

Height and spread: to 10m (33ft).
Hardiness: Frost hardy 9–10.
Cultivation: Grow in well-drained, fertile soil in sun or partial shade.

Ipomoea purpurea

Parthenocissus henryana

Jasminum officinale

Lonicera
Honeysuckle, woodbine

Many of these deciduous or evergreen woody climbers have fragrant, trumpet-like flowers and are perfect to cover a wall. L. japonica 'Halliana' (Zones 4–10) is evergreen and has white flowers that turn yellow. L. periclymenum (Zones 5–9) is best for fragrance: L. p. 'Serotina' has purple and red flowers from mid-summer to autumn.

Height and spread: 4m (13ft).
Hardiness: Fully hardy.
Cultivation: Grow in any soil in sun or partial shade, with the roots in shade. Make sure the soil does not dry out.

Parthenocissus
Boston ivy, Virginia creeper

Spectacular crimson autumn colour distinguishes these deciduous, vigorous, self-clinging climbers. The leaves grow in the most pleasing overlapping fashion, creating a fresh curtain even in shade. P. henryana (Zones 7–9) is probably the best form, with its deep green leaves and creamy white veins.

Height and spread: 10m (33ft).
Hardiness: Borderline to fully hardy 4–9.
Cultivation: Grow in well-drained soil in sun or shade.

Passiflora caerulea

Passiflora caerulea
Passion flower

This fast-growing climber has very exotic flowers. It is not reliably hardy, but could be grown as an annual. The flowers are white with a pink flush and a purple-banded crown of almost incredible complexity. They are then followed by soft orange fruits, which are edible but of dubious interest, unless you can use them to make the most memorable jam.

Height and spread: 3m (10ft).
Hardiness: Frost hardy 8–10.
Cultivation: Grow in fertile, well-drained soil in full sun with protection in winter.

Rosa
Rose

Roses are not usually very happy in containers, but if you want a beautiful rose as part of your roof garden, try growing one in as large a pot as possible and keep the potting mix well fed. The roses recommended here are all climbers. R. 'Madame Alfred Carrière' (Zones 5–9) has a mass of white, scented flowers and does not mind some shade. R. 'New Dawn' (Zones 4–9) has shiny, dark green leaves that complement perfectly the well-shaped, scented, pearl pink flowers, borne in clusters in summer and autumn. R. 'Guinée' (Zones 4–9) is the most perfect, velvety red rose, of astounding beauty and perfume.

Height and spread: to 5m (16ft).
Hardiness: Fully hardy.
Cultivation: Grow in a very fertile soil in sun or light shade. Deadhead when necessary. Prune regularly to keep their shape and to improve their longevity in a container.

Solanum
Potato vine

Two of these semi-evergreen scrambling climbers are good candidates for an exposed garden. S. crispum 'Glasnevin' (Zones 8–9) is extremely vigorous, with oval leaves and clusters of purple flowers with a yellow centre. S. jasminoides 'Album' (Zones 8–10) has white flowers produced over a long period in summer (and sometimes well into winter) against dark green leaves. Tiny purple berries are borne in autumn.

Rosa 'New Dawn'

Solanum jasminoides 'Album'

Height and spread: to 6m (20ft).
Hardiness: Frost hardy to frost tender.
Cultivation: Grow in fertile soil in sun. Cut plants back regularly to prevent them outgrowing their space. In harsh winters protect the pot with horticultural fleece and a dry mulch.

Thunbergia alata
Black-eyed Susan

This charming annual climber has heart-shaped leaves and small, flat flowers, orange-yellow with striking dark brown centres. It grows rapidly. Within a summer it will twine up an arch or clothe a pergola, or cascade down a wall or from a hanging basket, introducing a cottage-garden feel.
Height and spread: 3m (10ft).
Hardiness: Frost tender.
Cultivation: Grow in fertile soil in full sun. Keep moist and feed regularly .

Trachelospermum jasminoides
Chinese jasmine, star jasmine, confederate jasmine

The long, oval, dark green leaves of this evergreen climber grow into a dense curtain, providing a perfect backdrop for very fragrant white flowers that are borne in loose clusters in summer. These are followed by 15cm (6in) long pods, which grow in pairs, containing tufted seeds. It could be used to cover a fence or a wall near a door to get the full benefit of its scent.
Height and spread: to 9m (28ft).
Hardiness: Frost hardy 8–10.
Cultivation: Grow in fertile soil in partial shade. Tie the plant in at first.

Trachelospermum jasminoides

Wisteria sinensis

Spectacular, scented, mauve pea-like flowers are carried in long racemes among a profusion of fern-like mid-green leaves, followed by velvety pale green pods. This vigorous, deciduous climber looks best against a wall or twining its way up a structure, so allowing you to see the flowers from below. 'Alba' has white racemes up to 25cm (10in) long. A wisteria may take 5–10 years to bloom, so it is best to buy a plant already in bloom so that you know it is mature and can see what colour it is.
Height and spread: to 10m (33ft).
Hardiness: Fully hardy 5–9.
Cultivation: Grow in well-drained soil, not too rich, in sun or light shade. Prune any long shoots in late summer, and in winter cut back to the main woody frame to ensure good flowers that year.

Thunbergia alata

Wisteria sinensis

annuals and perennials

These are the plants that will "accessorize" your desired look. Whether you choose bright colours or gentle greens, the pleasure of watching the new growth emerging in spring and summer is hard to equal. Unless otherwise indicated, these plants require well-drained, fertile soil in full sun.

Agapanthus africanus

Campanula carpatica

Cleome

Cosmos 'Sensation'

Agapanthus

This clump-forming perennial has large umbels of white or blue trumpet-shaped flowers and strap-shaped leaves. The plants will produce increasing numbers of flowers as they get older. *A. africanus* (African lily) has deep blue flowers.
Height: 1m (3ft).
Spread: 50cm (20in).
Hardiness: Half hardy 9–10.
Cultivation: Grow in fertile soil, moist but well drained, in full sun. Mulch and insulate pots in winter.

Astrantia

Throughout the summer this clump-forming perennial produces long-lasting leaves of a lovely shape and jewel-like flowers. The flowers are greenish white (*A. major*), pink (*A. maxima*) and burgundy (*A. purpurea*).
Height: 60cm (2ft).
Spread: 30cm (12in).
Hardiness: Fully hardy 5–8.

Campanula
Bellflower

This very useful group comprises mainly blue bell-shaped or starry flowers of varying heights.
C. carpatica hugs the ground with open, cup-shaped, white or blue flowers. *C. medium* (Canterbury bell) is erect and evergreen, with wavy-edged leaves and spikes of bell-shaped white, blue and purple flowers in summer – invaluable as a gap filler. A rockery favourite, *C. poscharskyana* is low-growing, rampant and spreading, with an abundance of star-shaped violet flowers in summer. Campanulas are great self-seeders, appearing next season where you least expect them.
Height: 10–60cm (4–24in).
Spread: 30cm (12in)—indefinite.
Hardiness: All the varieties mentioned are fully hardy 4–7.
Cultivation: Grow in moist soil in semi-shade.

Cleome
Spider flower

Sown in situ in spring, this most satisfying annual will grow fast to produce a tall, bushy plant that is surmounted by a firework explosion of pink, mauve, purple and white spidery flowers. Planted in a group, they are sure to attract comment.
Height: to 1m (3ft).
Spread: 50cm (20in).
Hardiness: Half hardy to frost tender.
Cultivation: Stake the stems for extra strength in an exposed roof position where winds threaten.

Cosmos

This group comprises summer- and early autumn-flowering annuals and tuberous perennials. There are many named varieties of the annual form to be grown from seed, all with delicate feathery leaves. 'Purity' is pristine white, Sensation Mixed ranges from white to carmine, while *C. bipinnatus*

'Versailles Tetra' has wonderful dull pink flowers. The tuberous *C. atrosanguineus* has rich maroon flowers smelling of chocolate. It is a choice plant that is welcome in any scheme. Cosmos are invaluable for their very long flowering period and make excellent cut flowers.
Height: 60–90cm (2–3ft).
Spread: 60cm (2ft).
Hardiness: Frost hardy to frost tender.
Cultivation: *C. atrosanguineus* will survive mild winters if well protected.

Crocosmia
Montbretia

These corms produce long, sword-like leaves and brightly coloured tubular flowers carried on tall, arching stems. A group of the tall 'Lucifer', with its rich red flowers, will make the most striking splash in mid-summer, while the long-lasting, lance-shaped leaves will add texture to a border throughout

Crocosmia 'Lucifer'

Dahlia 'Bishop of Llandaff'

Geranium sanguineum

Helenium

most of the summer.
Height: 1m (3ft).
Spread: 30cm (12in).
Hardiness: Frost hardy 5–9.
Cultivation: In cold areas the corms should be lifted and stored for winter.

Dahlia

After many years of oblivion, dahlias have regained their popularity. These summer- and autumn-flowering perennial corms are available in many named varieties and a great range of colours, except for blues. The deep red 'Bishop of Llandaff', with its bronze leaves, is a great favourite of designers and gardeners. Most dahlias require protection in winter by storing the corms, so many people buy them as small plants in spring and treat them as annuals.
Height and spread: to 1m (3ft).
Hardiness: Frost hardy to frost tender.
Cultivation: Stake taller varieties.

Echinacea purpurea
Coneflower

This strong, summer-flowering perennial has long, dark green leaves and large, daisy-like flowers of the most vibrant pink with dark brown centres. They will look particularly dazzling planted in a group to face the sunset.
Height: 1m (3ft).
Spread: 50cm (20in).
Hardiness: Fully hardy 4–9.
Cultivation: Grow in any fertile, well-drained soil.

Euphorbia amygdaloides 'Purpurea'
Wood spurge

Euphorbia is a semi-evergreen perennial with narrow purple leaves and domed heads of red and yellow bracts in spring. Its striking colour and erect form make it a useful filler in a shady position. *E. griffithii* 'Fireglow' has orange-red flowers.
Height: 1m (3ft).

Spread: 50cm (20in).
Hardiness: Fully hardy 7–9.
Cultivation: Grow in moist, well-drained soil in sun or partial shade.

Gaura lindheimeri

The many slender, upright stems of this delicate-looking perennial emerge from a tuft of long, narrow, mid-green leaves and are covered with pink buds opening to star-shaped white flowers. It is worth growing for its very long flowering period (from midsummer until the first frosts) and for the way in which the little flowers resemble fluttering butterflies.
Height and spread: 1m (3ft).
Hardiness: Fully hardy 6–9.

Geranium
Cranesbill

This is such a huge group of perennials, some of which are evergreen, that there is always a variety flowering from early spring to late autumn. They are a must in any garden. One of the earliest to flower is the tall *G. phaeum* (Zones 4–9), with its maroon flowers, while the low-growing *G. sanguineum* (Zones 4–9) follows soon after with delicate pale pink flowers. *G.* 'Johnson's Blue' (Zones 4–9) has long been a great favourite with gardeners, while *G. macrorrhizum* (Zones 4–9) has very aromatic leaves; the flowers of 'album' are white and pink, 'Bevan's Variety' has magenta flowers. Finally, the spectacular *G. maderense* (Zones 9–10), a stately plant of deeply cut leaves and deep pink flowers, could be grown on its own in a large pot but would need total protection in winter.
Height: 15–90cm (6in–3ft).
Spread: 30–90cm (1–3ft).
Hardiness: *G. maderense* is half hardy; all others listed are fully hardy.
Cultivation: Grow in well-drained soil in sun or shade.

Helenium
Sneezeweed

This lovely perennial produces a mass of flowers for a long period in summer and autumn. Looking like small sunflowers, they have dark green foliage and branching stems carrying sprays of daisy-like flowers in a whole range of sunny colours, mostly bright yellow or orange. Some named varieties are worth hunting for, such as 'Moerheim Beauty', with rich red flowers, or 'Sunshine' in deep amber, mahogany and scarlet. 'Autumn Lollipop' has a very prominent dark brown centre, with a ring of small, rich yellow petals, making it a striking cut flower.
Height and spread: 60cm (2ft).
Hardiness: Most fully hardy 4–9.

Hemerocallis
Daylily

Trumpet-shaped flowers, each lasting for only one day, are borne in succession on this semi-evergreen perennial with long, arching leaves. There are a great number of named varieties to suit any colour scheme, in deep oranges, reds and creamy yellows, such as 'Jake Russell'.
Height and spread: 60–75cm (24–30in).
Hardiness: Most fully hardy 4–9.
Cultivation: Deadhead regularly to keep the plant looking good.

Hemerocallis 'Jake Russell'

Hosta

Knautia macedonica

Nicotiana

Hosta
Plantain lily

The luxuriant foliage of hostas grows in a rosette. The range of sizes and leaf shapes is impressive, while the colour can vary from brilliant green to buttery yellow to blue-grey. Pale purple flower spikes soar above the leaves in summer. It is well known that the fleshy leaves are a magnet for snails and slugs, but this is not a problem in pots up on a roof. Hostas are an almost essential addition to any planting scheme, since they enhance other colour combinations. Alternatively, they can be used on their own as specimen plants.

H. sieboldii has long green leaves edged in white; *H. sieboldiana* has big, veined, glaucous leaves, while *H. venusta* has small narrow leaves.

Height and spread: 2.5cm–1m (1in–3ft).

Hardiness: Fully hardy 4–9.

Cultivation: Grow in rich, moist but well-drained soil in shade.

Knautia macedonica

This perennial is currently very much in fashion, and justifiably so, since its flowers, which look like little pincushions, are of the most intense crimson on long, erect stems. They attract attention wherever they are planted, enhancing any other grouping but always starring.

Height: 90cm (3ft).

Spread: 75cm (30in).

Hardiness: Fully hardy 5–9.

Lavatera
Mallow

If sown in spring, the annual forms provide a long show of silky flowers from white to vibrant pink throughout the summer. New varieties are produced all the time, so it is wise to consult a reliable seed catalogue.

Height and spread: 30–90cm (1–3ft).

Hardiness: Most fully hardy.

Myosotis 'Blue Ball'
Forget-me-not

This biennial has bright blue flowers above long, narrow leaves. It is a joy in spring, as it forms a perfect carpet under spring bulbs.

Height and spread: 15cm (6in).

Hardiness: Fully hardy.

Nicotiana
Tobacco plant

Even in shady conditions, this well-loved garden annual produces a profusion of flowers over a long period. The best-known varieties are *N. x sanderae* Sensation Series, with scented flowers in varying colours from white to burgundy. *N. x s.* 'Lime Green' looks great in a white scheme, where the green flowers add a subtle note between the leaves and flowers of other plants. *N. sylvestris* is the great star of the family, rising up to a stately 1.5m (5ft) and producing white candelabras of scented flowers in late summer.

Height: 60cm–1.5m (2–5ft).

Spread: 30–90cm (1–3ft).

Hardiness: Most half hardy.

Cultivation: Support *C. sylvestris* with a circle of pea sticks.

Nigella damascena 'Miss Jekyll'
Love-in-a-mist

Seeds for this fast-growing, erect annual should be sown in situ. Blue flowers seem to float in a cloud of feathery, fresh green leaves, to be followed by dark seed pods, making this plant a wonderful filler.

N. d. 'Persian Pink' is a popular pink cultivar, and 'Persian Jewels' offers a mixture of colours (blue, pink, mauve and white). Dwarf blue forms are also available.

Height: 45cm (18in).

Spread: 20cm (8in).

Hardiness: Fully hardy.

Nigella damascena

Ophiopogon planiscapus
Mundo grass

This evergreen perennial is popular for its grass-like appearance. Grown in quantity over a large area, it will give the illusion of a lawn. It has small white flowers in summer. 'Nigrescens' is a very interesting form with black leaves, found in many contemporary schemes as a feature on its own or as ground-cover between grasses or phormiums.

Height: 15cm (6in).

Spread: 30cm (12in).

Hardiness: Fully hardy 6–10.

Cultivation: Grow in humus-rich soil in sun or shade.

Pelargonium

Whether you love them or consider them banal, pelargoniums are the quintessential plant for balconies and roof terraces. They are very good-natured, will withstand neglect and will respond with great gusto to minimal care. Their growing habit, trailing or upright, makes them perfect for single pots, and they are available with scarlet, white, pink or almost black flowers. The zonal varieties have very distinctive dark bands (zones) on their leaves. If well cared for, pelargoniums can flower continuously for up to 4 months.

Height and spread: 35–40cm (14–16in).

Hardiness: Almost all frost tender.

Cultivation: Deadhead and feed regularly throughout the summer.

Ophiopogon planiscapus

Phormium

Rudbeckia hirta

Sedum spectabile

Viola x wittrockiana

Phormium
New Zealand flax

This almost omnipresent perennial is of great value in any garden. Its soaring, lance-shaped leaves and its sheer bulk are invaluable as focal points to bring a touch of exoticism to a planting scheme, with the added bonus of their resilience to wind. Very long dark stems bearing exotic orange flowers appear in summer. *P. tenax* 'Dazzler' has glaucous leaves with an orange margin, while *P. t.* 'Purpureum' has leaves ranging from rich purple to dark copper.
Height: to 3m (10ft).
Spread: 1–2m (3–6ft).
Hardiness: Most frost hardy 9–10.
Cultivation: Grow in moist but well-drained soil in sun.

Polystichum aculeatum
Fern

Introducing beautiful and ancient ferns is a way of adding an element of stillness to a design. They grow best in woodlands but will be happy up in the sky under the shelter of a tree or in a shady corner. This species has broad, lacy, evergreen fronds forming a tall shuttlecock. It will not mind the wind.
Height: 60cm (2ft).
Spread: 75cm (30in).
Hardiness: Fully hardy 4–8.
Cultivation: Grow in moist, well-drained soil with plenty of fibrous organic matter in semi-shade. Cut back the old fronds in late winter to reveal new fronds unfurling in spring.

Rudbeckia hirta
Coneflower

This is one of the 'Prairie' perennials, which are widely used for creating big blocks of colour long into the autumn. 'Marmalade' has erect stems carrying rich, golden, daisy-like flowers with a prominent black centre over a mass of dark green leaves. 'Rustic Dwarfs' produces a profusion of large flowers in a mixture of tones from yellow to bronze to mahogany.
Height: to 60cm (2ft).
Spread: 30cm (12in).
Hardiness: Fully hardy.

Salvia
Sage

Salvias include a large group of annuals and perennials of immense value. Among the annual varieties *S. Splendens* 'Red Arrow' produces a mass of vivid red spikes on erect stems. *S. farinacea* has silvery stems, from which emerge hundreds of tiny blue flowers. *S. patens* has the most dazzling blue flowers, while the clary sage, *S. sclarea*, which was formerly believed to clear sight, is a biennial producing rosettes of leaves one year and a mass of branches covered with pink and white bracts the next. It is worth experimenting with salvias, as there is a variety suited to most colour schemes and designs.
Height and spread: to 60cm (2ft).
Hardiness: Frost hardy to fully hardy.
Cultivation: Grow in dry, well-drained soil in full sun.

Sedum spectabile
Ice plant

Above fleshy grey-green leaves, sedums produce large, flat, flowerheads, each composed of tiny fragrant pink flowers that are very attractive to butterflies. The flowers last a long time, glowing into the autumn light when most plants have finished flowering. They look equally good as part of a mixed planting or in a single pot.
Height and spread: 50cm (20in).
Hardiness: Fully hardy 4–9.
Cultivation: Grow in well-drained, even poor, soil in full sun.

Verbena bonariensis

This is a great eye-catcher, with purplish blue flowers carried on stiff stems high above a mass of dark green leaves. It appears to fill every spare space just where it is needed.
Height: 1.5m (5ft).
Spread: 60cm (2ft).
Hardiness: Frost hardy 7–10.

Viola

These delightfully old-fashioned annuals and perennials provide a huge range of colours. *V. cornuta* 'Boughton Blue' (Zones 5–8) has pure sky-blue flowers in summer. *V. tricolor* (Zones 3–8) has a dark purple top half and a yellow base, and is a profuse self-seeder. *V. x wittrockiana*, the garden pansy, has large flowers and is usually grown as an annual. Plants in the Floral Dance Series brave the winter winds and snow, always reappearing unscathed after the storm. *V. tricolor* 'Bowles' Black', the black pansy, rewards close inspection, as its small flowers sometimes get overshadowed by larger plants.
Height and spread: 10–15cm (4–6in).
Hardiness: Fully hardy.

Xeranthemum
Immortelle

Plants of this erect annual have narrow, silvery leaves and stiff stems surmounted by daisy-like, papery double flowers in lavender blue. Their good nature and long flowering time make them ideal gap-fillers. They were traditionally used as dried flowers, as their common name indicates.
Height: 60cm (2ft).
Spread: 45cm (18in).
Hardiness: Half hardy.

Zinnia

This very striking annual has large flowers and an excellent growing habit. Many new hybrids appear each year, but it is best to choose the simplest flowers, such as the Thumbelina Series or Pulcino Mixed, since the range of dazzling colours is sufficient decoration. They are most striking planted en masse to form an "embroidery" of clear and shocking pink, scarlet, gold and carmine.
Height and spread: 45cm (18in).
Hardiness: Tender.

bulbs

Dormant in the soil for several months, many bulbs appear reliably year after year, often when we have almost forgotten they were there. Bulbs are mainly associated with spring, but they can make an appearance from late winter to late autumn. Plants bulbs at a depth of two and a half times their height.

Allium caeruleum

Anemone blanda 'Atrocaerulea'

Camassia leichtlinii

Cyclamen hederifolium

Allium
Onion

Most alliums have narrow leaves and spheres of small flowers at the end of erect stems in summer, such as the blue *A. caeruleum* (Zones 4–10). *A. moly* (Zones 3–9) has a laxer, scented flower in a clear yellow. *A. schoenoprasum* (Zones 3–10), the edible chive, has small purple flowers with a dense clump of long thin leaves, very decorative to edge a large planter. The very tall purple *A.* 'Globemaster' has glossy leaves and towers over its neighbours.
Height: 15–90cm (6in–3ft).
Spread: 5–20cm (2–8in).
Hardiness: Frost to fully hardy.
Cultivation: Grow in well-drained soil in an open, sunny position.

Anemone
Windflower

The tiny, strangely shaped tubers of *A. blanda* 'White Splendour' (Zones 6–9) are best bought in large quantities to create a pure white carpet of small, daisy-like flowers above pretty leaves in early spring. *A. nemorosa* 'Robinsoniana' (Zones 4–8) produces pretty pale blue flowers with a grey tinge on the outside.
Height: 5–10cm (2–4in).
Spread: 10–15cm (4–6in).
Hardiness: Fully hardy.
Cultivation: Grow in humus-rich soil in sun or partial shade.

Camassia leichtlinii

This American native is easy to grow and is invaluable in a shady corner. A mat of long, narrow leaves covers the soil, from which rise strong stems carrying spikes of starry flowers in summer. 'Alba' has white flowers with a green tinge, while the Caerulea Group has dark blue flowers.
Height: 70–90cm (28–36in).
Spread: 20–30cm (8–12in).
Hardiness: Frost hardy 3–10.
Cultivation: Grow in humus-rich soil in partial shade.

Crocus

These small, fragrant goblets announce the arrival of spring in such an array of colours that it seems almost impossible to recommend any particular variety. It might be best to refer to a reliable bulb supplier and choose from among such species as *C. angustifolius* (yellow and bronze) *C. tommasinianus* (pale cobalt inside and silvery grey outside) or *C. t.* 'Ruby Giant' (deep violet). Crocuses not only herald spring; some flower in autumn, and these are often taller than the spring varieties. The leaves appear separately, in spring. Among these, *C. speciosus*, either in white ('Albus') or pale lilac ('Artabir'), would light up a grey day. *C. sativus* is the saffron crocus.
Height: 5–15cm (2–6in).
Spread: 2.5–5cm (1–2in).
Hardiness: Most fully hardy 3–8.
Cultivation: Grow in well-drained soil in sun.

Cyclamen hederifolium

This low-growing perennial is happy in the shade of other plants and a great joy to discover peeping through in late autumn. The swept-back petals are pale pink with a dark red mark at the base, and the leaves have silvery markings. Left undisturbed, they will self-seed freely, often appearing where you least expect them.
Height and spread: 10cm (4in).
Hardiness: Fully hardy 5–9.
Cultivation: Grow in humus-rich, well-drained soil in sun or partial shade.

Hyacinthoides non-scripta
English bluebell

These nodding blue flowers, with their glossy, strap-shaped leaves and honeyed scent, are a true symbol of spring.
Height: 20–40cm (8–16in).
Spread: 8–10cm (3–4in).
Hardiness: Fully hardy 6–9.
Cultivation: Grow in moist soil, with organic matter, in partial shade.

Leucojum aestivum

Leucojum aestivum
Summer snowflake
At first glance these could appear to be giant snowdrops overstaying their winter slot. They have nodding white bells, more open with green tips than snowdrops. They provide a robust display in shade in early summer, with long, dark green leaves.
Height: to 1m (3ft).
Spread: to 12cm (5in).
Hardiness: Fully hardy 4–9.
Cultivation: Grow in moist, rich soil in a shady position.

Lilium
Lily
Planted in layers in large, deep pots, lilies will grow in a dense mass to create a succession of spectacular shows with the headiest of scents. For pure majestic beauty, the white *L. candidum* (Madonna lily) is well loved, as is *L. regale*, whose large, trumpet-shaped flowers are white inside and purple outside. *L.* 'Pink Perfection' is a deep purple-pink with long trumpets; *L. tigrinum* (Tiger lily) has deep orange recurved petals.
Height: 1m (3ft).
Spread: 30cm (12in).
Hardiness: All listed are fully hardy 4–9.
Cultivation: Grow in humus-rich soil in sun. Good drainage is essential.

Muscari
Grape hyacinth
These small bulbs make a delightful edge to a long planter or a tight group in a shallow bowl. Their long-lasting, narrow leaves appear in spring before the clusters of tiny purple flowers. *M. armeniacum* is the most commonly grown form; *M. neglectum* has blue-black flowers rimmed with white.
Height: to 20cm (8in).
Spread: 5cm (2in).
Hardiness: Fully hardy 2–9.
Cultivation: Grow in any well-drained soil in sun or light shade.

Narcissus
Daffodil
Choose any species indicated as "good for naturalizing". 'Thalia' has three pure white flowers at the end of each stem. The cyclamineus group has some very good short varieties, such as 'February Gold', 'Little Witch' or 'Jack Snipe'. The dwarf 'Tête à Tête' has long been a favourite, with its multi-headed, golden flowers, as has the taller *N. poeticus recurvus* (Old pheasant's eye), an enchanting, fragrant, glistening white flower with a yellow centre edged in dark red.
Height: 15cm (6in) for dwarf forms; to 45cm (18in) for *N. poeticus*.
Hardiness: Most are fully hardy 3–9.
Cultivation: Grow in well-drained soil, preferably in full sun.

Nectaroscordum siculum
This might look like a rare plant, but it is, in fact, easy to grow. The long, thin, erect leaves are shorter than the tall stems, which support groups of nodding, bell-shaped flowers of the most interesting green tone, with maroon and yellow markings. A group will attract attention in early summer above emerging hostas.
Height: to 1m (3ft).
Spread: 30cm (12in).
Hardiness: Fully hardy 7–10.
Cultivation: Grow in well-drained soil in sun or partial shade.

Scilla
Squill
Planted in large groups, these small bulbs will bring blues back into the growing palette. They have glossy leaves and bell-shaped flowers, pale sky blue for *S. mischtschenkoana* or deepest blue for *S. siberica* 'Spring Beauty'.
Height: 10cm (4in).
Spread: 5cm (2in).
Hardiness: Fully hardy 1–8.
Cultivation: Grow in well-drained soil in sun or partial shade.

Tulipa
Tulip
A must for any roof terrace, among the most remarkable hybrids are the highly desirable black tulip 'Queen of Night', the green-striped white tulip 'Spring Green', and 'White Triumphator', with its elegant pointed petals. Dwarf forms are very useful in containers, and most of the species tulips will be excellent choices, particularly the *T. humilis* group or the bright red *T. praestans* 'Fusilier', or *T. tarda*, with its bronze petals opening to pale yellow and white. 'China Pink', one of the lily-flowered group, looks ravishing above a carpet of forget-me-nots (*Myosotis*), while some tulips will have not only bicoloured flowers but also beautifully marked leaves, such as 'Oriental Beauty' or 'Plaisir'.
Height: 10–50cm (4–20in).
Hardiness: Fully hardy 3–8.
Cultivation: Grow in any well-drained soil in sun.

Zantedeschia
Arum lily, calla lily
The long-lasting, lush leaves of these exotic-looking tuberous plants would be reason enough to grow them. But they also produce striking, funnel-shaped spathes (bracts) enclosing a cluster of tiny flowers (spadix). The well-known arum lily, *Z. aethiopica* (Zones 8–10), has white flowers, while the striking *Z. elliottiana* (Zone 10) has leaves spotted with silver and a pure yellow flower. The extraordinary looking *Z. aethiopica* 'Green Goddess' has a large white flower heavily splashed with green.
Height: 45cm–1m (18–36in.)
Spread: to 60cm (2ft).
Hardiness: Frost hardy to frost tender.
Cultivation: Grow in well-drained soil in sun or partial shade. For better protection keep the crown 15cm (6in) below the soil surface.

Lilium regale

Tulipa 'Queen of Night'

Zantedeschia aethiopica

grasses

In addition to the expected green, grasses are also available in blue, blue-grey or bright red, and can vary from little tufts to big, splashy fountains, most with interesting flowers. But their greatest asset on a roof terrace is the way in which they move with the slightest hint of a breeze.

Briza media
Quaking grass

This is an evergreen, tuft-forming perennial grass. The mid-green leaves are topped in summer by a great number (up to 30) of purple, drooping spikelets that last well into winter. They can also be dried to make excellent decorations.
Height: 30–60cm (1–2ft).
Spread: 8–10cm (3–4in).
Hardiness: Fully hardy 5–9.

Cultivation: Grow in well-drained soil in sun.

Carex

This evergreen sedge is low-growing and clump-forming, very useful as a textured ground-cover. *C. buchananii* (Zones 6–9) has narrow, copper-coloured leaves, tinged red at the base, and brown spikelets. *C. elata* (Zones 5–9) has somewhat glaucous leaves, and its

Carex elata

triangular stems bear blackish-brown spikelets during the summer. *C. grayi* (Zones 3–8) has bright green leaves and white flowers in summer.
Height: to 40cm (16in).
Spread: to 1m (3ft).
Hardiness: Fully to frost hardy.
Cultivation: Grow in rich, moist soil in shade or partial shade.

Cortaderia selloana
Pampas grass

This is the queen of all grasses, forming a majestic, evergreen fountain of shimmering narrow leaves up to 1m (3ft) long. In summer, very tall plumes of white spikelets tower above the leaves, and remain for a long time.
Height: to 2m (6ft).
Spread: 1.2m (4ft).
Hardiness: Fully hardy.
Cultivation: Grow in deep, fertile soil in full sun. To avoid a mound of dead stems in the centre of the plant and to keep it happy in its container, prune hard in spring and do not allow it to dry out.

Deschampsia cespitosa

Deschampsia cespitosa
Tufted hair grass

This evergreen, tuft-forming grass forms a dense mass of narrow, rough-edged, dark green leaves, with dainty, pale brown spikelets in summer that last well into winter.
Height: to 1m (3ft).
Spread: 30cm (12in).
Hardiness: Fully hardy 5–9.
Cultivation: Grow in well-drained soil in sun or shade.

Festuca glauca
Blue fescue

This plant is an evergreen, perennial, tuft-forming grass. It is grown for its narrow leaves in various shades of blue-green to silvery white, creating a striking contrast to a very deep purple plant such as *Ophiopogon planiscapus* 'Nigrescens'. It bears panicles of spikelets in summer.
Height: to 30cm (12in).
Spread: 25cm (10in)
Hardiness: Fully hardy 4–8.
Cultivation: Grow in well-drained soil in sun or shade.

Cortaderia selloana

Festuca glauca

Luzula nivea
Snowy woodrush

This slow-spreading, evergreen, perennial rush has leaves edged with white hairs and dense clusters of prominent white flowers in early summer. By contrast, *L. sylvatica* has thin leaves and delicate, arching, dark brown flowers in clusters.
Height: 60cm (2ft).
Spread: 45cm (18in).
Hardiness: Fully hardy 4–9.
Cultivation: Grow in cool, humus-rich soil in full sun.

Melica altissima 'Atropurpurea'

This evergreen, tuft-forming grass has broad green leaves with short hairs underneath, but its interest lies in the long, narrow, purple spikelets that hang from the top of its tall stems in summer.
Height: to 2m (6ft).
Spread: 60cm (2ft).
Hardiness: Fully hardy 6–9.
Cultivation: Grow in humus-rich soil in sun or partial shade.

Miscanthus sinensis

This grass grows up to 3m (10ft) in one season. Its mid-green leaves turn bronze in autumn and last well into winter. 'Gracillimus' has very thin leaves, while 'Zebrinus' is often chosen for its distinctive yellowish-white ring markings. Both may bear fan-shaped panicles of hairy white flowers in autumn. They need strong summer heat in order to flower.
Height: 1.2–3m (4–10ft).
Spread: 50cm (20in).
Hardiness: Fully hardy 5–10.
Cultivation: Grow in any soil in sun or partial shade.

Panicum virgatum 'Rubrum'
Old-witch grass, switch grass

This annual grass has broad leaves and hairy stems. The leaves are green at first, then turn red in late summer, and there are long panicles of tiny, brown, feathery spikelets.
Height: to 1.2m (4ft).
Spread: 75cm (30in).
Hardiness: Fully hardy 5–9.
Cultivation: Grow in any good soil in full sun.

Pennisetum villosum
Feathertop

This herbaceous grass forms a tuft of narrow leaves with long flowering stems bearing panicles of very hairy white spikelets. These have a pink tinge in autumn before turning brown.
Height: 1m (3ft).
Spread: 50cm (20in).
Hardiness: Frost hardy 8–10.
Cultivation: Grow in rich soil in sun.

Stipa gigantea
Golden oats

This evergreen grass has rather unremarkable long, floppy leaves. In late spring, however, it produces the most amazing display: an abundance of tall, elegant flowers, like tiny shards of silver, with long, golden tails that catch the light like jewels. You will need room to do it justice.
Height: 2.5m (8ft).
Spread: 1m (3ft).
Hardiness: Fully hardy 5–9
Cultivation: Grow in light, fertile soil in full sun.

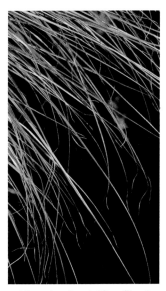

Miscanthus sinensis 'Gracillimus'

Panicum virgatum

Penisetum villosum

alpines and succulents

These plants can provide the finishing touches to your roof garden, adding elements of pure fascination. Alpines will be at ease high up, oblivious to storms and cold weather, as long as they are not wet. Many succulents are fully hardy and thrive in the strong light of the roof garden.

Agave americana 'Mediopicta Alba'

Dianthus myrtinervius

Agave americana
Century plant, maguey

Although rather tender, this succulent is worth growing if it can be protected in winter or if you live in a warm area. It produces a rosette of fleshy, blue-grey leaves with toothed edges and needle-like points. This might be a hazard in a confined space, but the agave could be grown in a large, tall pot in a well-defined area. The spectacular flower spikes are infrequent, and their absence usually means that the central rosettes have died, but, since the plant will have freely produced small rosettes all around the pot, these can easily be detached and potted on to produce new plants for the future. 'Mediopicta Alba' has central yellow stripes along its leaves.

Height and spread: to 2m (6ft).
Hardiness: Frost tender 9–10.
Cultivation: Grow in standard cactus potting mix in full sun.

Dianthus
Pink

These delightful flowers will cover the ground with a splash of colour and many will ravish you with their fragrance. There are many different hybrids to choose from, so it is a question of personal taste.
D. carthusianorum has cherry-pink flowers growing among a mound of evergreen, grass-like leaves.
D. 'Pike's Pink' is low-growing, with grey-green evergreen foliage and a mass of fragrant double pink flowers, while *D. plumarius* 'Ipswich Pink Mixed' produces a wonderful collection of pink, red, white and mauve flowers above the dense blue foliage.

Height: 5–9cm (2–3in).
Spread: 20cm (8in).
Hardiness: Fully hardy 5–7.
Cultivation: Grow in slightly alkaline, free-draining soil, in an open, sunny position.

Gaultheria procumbens

Decorative combinations of colours at different times of the year make this vigorous, ground-hugging evergreen worth a place in your garden. In summer, single white bells are followed by scarlet berries, and in winter, some of the oval, dark green, leathery leaves turn red. Both these stages often seem to happen simultaneously, making this plant an attractive, eye-catching ground-cover, particularly in a dark corner of the roof terrace.

Height: 5–15cm (2–6in).
Spread: Indefinite.
Hardiness: Fully hardy 3–8.
Cultivation: Grow in moist ericaceous (acid) soil in shade or semi-shade.

Persicaria vacciniifolia
Knotweed

This evergreen, mat-forming ground-cover is sometimes considered too invasive in a garden, but it is much easier to control when grown in containers. The combination of the fresh green leaves taking on a red tinge in autumn, and the orderly pink spikes in late summer, make this plant a very useful gap-filler that should not be overlooked.

Height: 10–15cm (4–6in).
Spread: to 30cm (12in).
Hardiness: Fully hardy 4–8.
Cultivation: Grow in well-drained soil in sun or shade.

Raoulia haastii

Use this ground-hugging succulent to tumble over a pot, or grow it alone in a shallow bowl to create a pool of vivid green in spring, turning chocolate brown in winter. It may have tiny yellow flowers in summer.

Height: 1cm (½in).

Spread: 25cm (10in).

Hardiness: Frost hardy 7.

Cultivation: Grow in gritty, well-drained, humus-rich soil in sun or partial shade.

Sedum

This genus includes many mat-forming rock plants with tiny fleshy leaves, good for ground-cover in a gravel area or in shallow terracotta bowls, where their red tinged leaves and tiny flat flowers can be admired in summer. Choose from *S. cauticola*, *S. ewersii* and *S. kamtschaticum*.

Height: 5cm (2in).

Spread: 15cm (6in)—indefinite.

Hardiness: All listed are fully hardy 5–9.

Cultivation: Grow in gritty, free-draining soil in full sun.

Sempervivum
Houseleek

The perfect geometry of their rosettes, as well as the orderly way in which they spread, make this most pleasing group of evergreen, mat-forming perennials a constant source of fascination. Added to this are the extraordinary changes of colour of their tiny leaves and the surprising flowers that rise from the rosettes on tall stems in yellows, reds and dull pinks. They have long been a great favourite and certainly should be grown on a roof, where they thrive in the strong light. In *S. arachnoideum*, the fleshy, red-tipped leaves are covered in white webs, looking magical after the rain, and the loose clusters of summer flowers are rose-red. *S. tectorum* has the best-coloured tiny, rose-pink stars. In summer, it has clusters of star-shaped, reddish-purple flowers on long stems.

Height: 8–15cm (3–6in).

Spread: 10–20cm (4–8in).

Hardiness: Fully hardy 5–9.

Cultivation: Grow in gritty, free-draining soil in full sun.

Veronica prostrata
Prostrate speedwell

If a splash of brilliant blue is required, the easy-natured, rapid-spreading speedwells can be relied on. The mat-forming species are particularly useful in softening up unsightly edges. Above small, oval leaves, spikes of the brightest blue saucer-shaped flowers appear in summer to cover the soil very effectively. 'Kapitan' has deep blue flowers, while 'Spode Blue' has pale blue flowers.

Height: to 30cm (12in) in flower.

Spread: Indefinite.

Hardiness: Fully hardy 4–7.

Cultivation: Grow in well-drained soil in sun.

Sempervivum tectorum

Sedum kamtschaticum

Veronica prostrata

edible plants

Home-grown fruit and vegetables are always something to be proud of, and they represent even more of a triumph when they are grown in the challenging environment of a roof garden. Whether you opt for just a few pots or a productive potager, there are many suitable crops to choose from.

Courgettes (*Cucurbita pepo*)

Potatoes (*Solanum tuberosum*)

Runner beans (*Phaseolus coccineus*)

Swiss chard (*Beta vulgaris*)

Vegetables

A great array of vegetables can be grown in pots or raised beds, benefiting from the strong light and heat on the roof in summer. They must be watered and fed regularly with either a chemical or organic fertilizer, best used as a root drench.

Aubergine (eggplant)
Solanum melongena

This plant is very decorative when the deep purple shiny fruits hang among the pale green leaves. The aubergines should be harvested regularly from midsummer to early autumn, or the plant will need staking. The variety 'Black Enorma F1 Hybrid' is particularly prolific.

Carrot
Daucus carota

Carrots can be sown in succession for harvesting throughout the year. 'Flyaway' is an early cropper bred for resistance to carrot root fly; 'Bertan' is a very sweet later variety, while the pest-resistant 'Jeanette F1 Hybrid' has a conical shape and lots of foliage, making it easy to pull.

Courgette (zucchini)
Cucurbita pepo

If these are sown in pots in spring, kept at 21°C (70°F) and planted outside in early summer, they will then be ready for harvesting in 50–65 days, depending on the varieties. Shiny green courgettes follow trumpet-like yellow flowers under large leaves, the whole plant being highly decorative. Good varieties include the round 'De Nice à Fruit Rond', yellow 'Gold Rush', and 'Dundoo F1 Hybrid'.

Pepper
Capsicum species

Sweet (bell) peppers should be started indoors and brought out in full sun in late spring. They are excellent for use on the barbecue. Varieties include 'California Wonder', the long, pointed 'Tasty Grill' red and yellow F1 Hybrid and 'Sweet Spanish mixed'. The related hot chilli peppers include 'Hungarian Wax', with beautifully shaped yellow fruit, the very hot 'Thai Dragon' and the highly decorative 'Firecracker', which looks like a string of fairylights.

Potato
Solanum tuberosum

To avoid storage problems, it is probably best to buy sprouted tubers, which can be planted in large deep tubs or square containers made of strong black plastic. The taste of fresh new potatoes, such as the 'Charlotte' variety or 'Belle de Fontenay', is hard to equal.

Radish
Raphinus

This can be sown every three weeks for a constant supply of fresh-tasting radishes such as 'Flamboyant Sabina' or 'French Breakfast 3'.

Runner (green) bean
(Phaseolus coccineus)

These plants are a great asset to any garden. Trained up a series of tripods made of bamboos, they will create wonderful green screens punctuated by bright red flowers, and produce long green beans, as in 'Lady Di', which are completely stringless, or 'Scarlet Emperor', throughout the summer months.

Swiss chard
Beta vulgaris Cicla Group

This vegetable is so decorative that it is worth growing for its appearance alone. The large, dark green, glossy leaves have a creamy white stem, while the ruby chard variety has the most dazzling red stem. One variety, 'Bright Lights', even combines a range of coloured stems (from white to pink, violet, orange and gold) with a delicious sweet taste and lots of nutrients.

Tomato
Lycopersicon esculentum

This is the ideal and most satisfactory roof-garden crop, as tomato plants love the strong sunshine and are very happy in containers or growing bags. Home-grown cherry tomatoes are sweet as well as decorative, and probably the best choice here would be varieties such as 'Balconi Red' or 'Sakura F1 Hybrid'. 'Tigerella' has pretty fruit with yellow stripes, and the award-winning 'Tomato Ruby' has long trusses of small fruit.

Herbs and salad leaves

Most herbs and salads can be grown in containers and so are suitable for a roof terrace. Fresh herbs for cooking and fresh-tasting salads would be reward enough, but the plants are also decorative.

Herbs such as the popular rosemary (*Rosmarinus*), thyme (*Thymus*), green and purple basil (*Ocimum basilicum* and *O. b.* 'Purple Ruffle'), oregano (*Origanum*), marjoram (*Origanum majorana*), coriander (cilantro) (*Coriandrum sativum*) and parsley (*Petroselinum crispum*) can be grown in terracotta pots or galvanized

planters. Mint (*Mentha*), delicious for mint tea, should be grown on its own as it tends to be very invasive. Chives (*Allium schoenoprasum*) make a wonderful edging and have the added advantage of pretty pink flowers in summer.

Salad leaves suitable for growing on the roof include all types of lettuce, particularly the cut and come again types, such as 'Bionda Foglia', corn salad (ready to pick a week from sowing) or 'Little Gem' — a dwarf variety that "hearts" quickly. Rocket (arugula) (*Eruca vesicaria*), which has pretty flowers, can be sown all through the summer

for a prolific and pungent salad, but it can easily go to seed.

Fruit

As we have seen previously, fruit trees can be grown on the roof, either espaliered against a wall or trained into a low cordon to act as decoration, and can also be productive. Some soft fruit can also be grown in containers.

Fig
Ficus carica
These are highly suitable trees as they grow into wonderfully decorative shapes, have beautiful leaves, and thrive in containers. To ripen, the figs need a good amount of hot sunshine for a long period, so it is best to remove any fruit appearing late in the season.

Fig (*Ficus carica*)

Ocimum basilicum

Grapevine
Vitis vinifera
This can be grown purely as a decorative feature trained over a pergola or an arch for the shape of its leaves and autumn colour. To harvest the grapes, prune all the long leaf shoots back to the main stem. Among the white varieties, 'Moscato bianco' ripens late in the season, while 'Moscato d'Amburgo', a red grape, ripens earlier.

Strawberry
Fragaria x *ananassa*
The wild strawberry (*F. vesca*) can be successfully grown as a ground-cover plant with the added bonus of bright red, small, tasty fruit. Larger fruit, such as 'Sarian F1 Hybrid' or 'Red Gauntlet', can cascade down the sides of a traditional strawberry pot all through the summer, providing many delicious desserts for the table.

Mixed salad leaves

Wild strawberry (*Fragaria vesca*)

site concerns and constraints

There is no other area of landscaping where the relationship between design and construction details is so interdependent as on a roof terrace. This is why, before any designing and construction can start, the roof has to be assessed for:

- building regulations – height and safety
- structure
- load-bearing capacity
- waterproofing
- access

building regulations

Whether you have purchased an apartment in a new development or an older building, you will need to be aware of the local building regulations if you intend to do any major work on the roof, as issues of maximum height allowed and safety regulations will be involved, and these vary greatly within and between states and countries. If you are using an architect and/or landscape architect, they will deal with these matters as part of their brief; if you are planning the work yourself, then your local planning department should be able to help.

structure

Whether you are living in a new or old building, it is essential to hire the services of a structural engineer in order to find out the nature of the structure you are dealing with. A local professional institute will be able to recommend an engineer in your area. If the building is new, provisions may have been made for the construction of a garden on the roof regarding access and reinforcement of peripheral areas.

load-bearing capacity

One of the main considerations will be how much weight is allowed on the roof. For this you need to distinguish between the "dead load" and the "live load". The former includes the roof

above left *Unless the roof has been built as a terrace, all the outlets for heating, ventilation and air-conditioning will have to be worked around or integrated into the design.*

left *This bamboo fence enclosing a small Japanese roof garden fits so perfectly with the design that it is hard to guess that it is made out of metal and hides ugly pipes.*

left *Erecting a large pergola on a roof requires the builder to find out the load-bearing capacity of the roof as well as where to fix the uprights for safety. The problem has been solved here by using fibreglass pillars and by stepping up the deck to allow for the column footings.*

structure itself and any permanent elements, such as ventilation and air-conditioning equipment. The "live load" includes human occupants, furnishings and plants. The design and construction of the roof garden will be completely tied to the permitted weights. You must also be careful to avoid grouping heavy items, such as planters or furniture, in one area to cause uneven stress.

If you have a balcony that projects, rather than being supported by a solid series of balconies below, it will probably be even less able to bear heavy loads.

waterproofing

The waterproofing of the roof is another essential factor to consider. A suitable waterproof membrane should have been installed when the building was constructed. It is then the responsibility of the garden designer or owner to develop a design that will not damage the waterproof membrane and will contribute to its longest possible life.

access

Roof terraces might be difficult to access, particularly in an old building with narrow stairs and no lift (elevator). This might impose great limitations on the design of a garden, which would involve bringing up heavy loads of building materials and plants. Priority would have to be given to choosing suitable light materials.

A flat roof is often an exit route in case of fire, which means that other occupants of the building must be able to reach it easily. Large pots or items of furniture should therefore not be placed too near doors and windows, so leaving a large space clear for people in the event of an emergency evacuation.

above *Access to a roof terrace is a very important consideration, not only for everyday use but also for when it is needed as an emergency escape route.*

top right *An antique door backed with mirrors has been cleverly inserted into this wooden privacy screen to give the illusion of a space beyond.*

design choices and constraints

The ultimate aim of the design is to create an outdoor roof space that can be enjoyed. What cannot be forgotten is that the roof is usually very exposed to the elements, as well as very visible, and it is important to work with these special conditions rather than ignoring them, so that they become an integral part of the design.

wind

It is important to know the direction of the prevailing wind in your area, though you should also be aware that, if you live in a city, its direction will probably be modified by surrounding roofs and buildings. In some cases they might shelter your terrace from harsh breezes, but in other situations they may actually increase the effect, even funnelling the wind in your direction. It is only with this knowledge that you can sensibly plan how to cope with the wind.

● Windbreaks should be securely attached to parts of the structure, such as parapet walls or the building walls.

● In the case of a new building, it may be possible to build sheltering structures on to the roof slabs before the waterproofing membrane is laid. This should be discussed with the architect or builder.

● Solid windbreaks will cause wind turbulence and pockets of cold air – they should either have holes at regular intervals or be made of something permeable, like hedging or mesh.

● Furniture must be sufficiently heavy so that it will not be blown around, or even right off, the roof, potentially causing great damage. If solid timber or metal (both heavy choices) are not desired, then any lighter materials must be securely attached to the terrace without affecting the waterproofing membrane.

drainage

The falls on the roof have to be particularly well thought out, as any water that is allowed to stand on the roof will inevitably affect the waterproofing. Assuming that the structural falls have been worked out by the architect beforehand, they must be respected when laying paving or decking on top of the slab, so that all the surface water can drain freely towards the guttering or gullies. Any outlet to the downpipes should be covered with a fine mesh to prevent any clogging with leaves or debris.

above This beautiful bespoke curved screen made of metal mesh is an elegant way of creating a transparent windbreak.

right To hide an unattractive fence, a screen of split willow can be bought off-the-shelf in a roll and attached with wire.

opposite left It is important to choose solid furniture to stay out on the roof, as anything light could easily fly off in a high wind, causing possible injury or damage.

cables and pipes

Electrical cables for lighting, water pumps and use of equipment such as music centres and computers, and pipes for irrigation and/or water features, will be more difficult to hide on a roof terrace than in a garden on the ground. If these services are not already present, it is therefore important to establish where they will be needed at the very beginning of the design process, as they can then be threaded under timber decking or incorporated within the construction of any paved areas.

storage

This is always a difficult problem to solve in any garden: where to put tools and all the other paraphernalia of gardening as well as covers for furniture if they have been used in winter. On a roof terrace, where everything is easily seen, it is even more of a problem.

● A storage seat with a hinged top, built along the same principles as a planter, and matching existing planters in size and style, could provide hidden space for tools, gardening gloves, fertilizers and a host of useful items. A pair would offer even more space.

● A large pot could be used to contain a hose or bags of potting mix.

● A far corner of the roof terrace could be screened by a hedge or a row of tall pots to hide a low timber or metal box, now sold in garden centres for storage purposes. This must be securely attached to the roof.

● A small shed could even be built as a lean-to against the parapet or building wall.

top right This storage unit, which is big enough for a bicycle, has been built on to the deck out of painted timber, using metal trays for planting, here containing ivy, to form the roof.

right A beautifully shaped pot of generous proportions could be left unplanted and used as a storage place for small garden equipment, a length of hose, or some potting mix.

plant care and maintenance

top To achieve lush growth like this on a windy, exposed terrace, very frequent watering will be needed in summer.

above This custom-made timber planter is slightly raised on small pieces of wood to ensure ventilation and better drainage and also to protect the deck.

Before thinking about plant care on a roof garden, it is of course essential to choose plants that can tolerate wind and strong light. If sheltered areas can be created, more delicate plants can be grown, but it is always best to opt for plants that will enjoy the conditions — and there are plenty of these to choose from — rather than trying to grow things that will never really thrive.

pots

Assuming that weight and structural issues have been considered, pots have to be large enough to allow healthy growth, particularly for trees and large shrubs, whose root systems can become quite extensive (though see advice on root pruning, below). Once a large container has been filled with potting mix and plants, the pot will be much too heavy to move, so make sure that large pots are placed where they do not obstruct any fire exit or services. If a container will need to be moved, it should be on some form of low trolley.

For ventilation and improved drainage, it is best to raise the pots slightly off the ground. For terracotta pots, small, custom-made terracotta feet are ideal for this purpose. For pots made of other materials, leftover tiles or scraps of wood from the decking could be neatly cut and placed on the floor before the pot is lowered into place on top of them.

planting and maintenance

To keep the weight to a minimum, a thick layer of drainage such as Lecca (expanded clay balls) should be placed at the bottom of any planter. This should be covered by a synthetic filter fabric, which will stop the potting mix that lies on top from seeping through and blocking the drainage.

The planting medium should not be ordinary garden soil but a lightweight, humus-rich potting mix. Garden centres supply bags of proprietary potting mix for containers. To make the mix even lighter and to keep it aerated, the addition of expanded volcanic rock has proved invaluable. In fact, some very successful ecological experiments have been made whereby plants are grown only in varying depths of expanded rock, which also acts as insulation, using organic fertilizers to give the plants their necessary nutrients. This development has important implications for roof terrace owners, who always have to be so conscious of the weight factor. A lightweight growing medium could mean that a much wider choice of containers is now available, and will also make transporting the medium up to the roof terrace much easier.

Fertilizing is vital on a roof garden, where all the plants are grown in containers. A slow-release fertilizer is best for plants in containers, though shrubs and trees will benefit from a steady release mixture, supplemented by a general-purpose liquid feed during the growing season. A liquid feed is also essential for healthy annuals and perennials. To improve the quality of the soil in the container, a layer of potting mix 10–15cm (4–6in) deep should be removed every other year and replaced with fresh potting mix.

Mulching is a good idea, as it is an excellent way of retaining moisture. Lack of water retention is a problem for any container-grown plant, but plants on the roof are affected even more because of the increased amount of sun and wind. A thick mulch will not only form a barrier against the elements, keeping the water trapped below it, but will also anchor the potting mix so that it does not get blown out of the containers.

Some gardeners advocate root pruning to keep trees healthy and happy in their planters. A quarter of the root ball is uncovered and sawn off every year, while still in its pot, and new potting mix is added. This might seem drastic, but it is an effective method of curbing growth and does not harm the plants.

Ordinary pruning is important for keeping plants in shape and encouraging new growth, and it is another method of preventing shrubs growing to the point where they are too big for their pots.

Keeping shrubs and trees well trimmed above ground and free of pests is another way of making sure that they can have a long and healthy life in confined conditions.

Supporting plants in these windy conditions is vital. For small plants, stakes attached to a wall or sunk into the container will be sufficient, but larger ones will need a more sturdy support, attached or free-standing, to protect their stems from breaking.

Finally, watering is an essential element in the care of any plants, but particularly those living on a windy terrace under strong sunlight. Make sure there is an outdoor tap by the terrace, and buy a length of garden hose long enough to reach all the plants. Watering will be a daily activity in the summer, so, if this will be too onerous, or if the owners of the terrace are frequently away, a computer-operated irrigation system should be installed.

right This very large London roof terrace has been carefully planted and nurtured over 20 years, and shows how much can successfully be grown on a roof, from mature trees and shrubs to a plethora of perennials and annuals.

below A low bed has been made out of timber and filled with perennials, which thrive under the shelter of the tall hedge behind it.

suppliers

UNITED KINGDOM

Architectural Plants
Cooks Farm, Nuthurst, Horsham,
West Sussex RH13 6LH.
Tel: 01403 891772
www.architecturalplants.com
Great range of accent plants

Clifton Nurseries
5a Clifton Villas, London W9 2PH.
Tel: 020 7289 6851
www.clifton.co.uk
Design, ornaments, pots and plants

The Conran Shop
Michelin House, 81 Fulham Road
London SW3 6RD.
Tel: 020 7589 7401
www.conran.com
Contemporary furniture, containers

Europlants
Great North Road, Bell Bar,
Hatfield, Herts, AL9 6DA.
Tel: 01707 649996
email: eurosales@europlants.net
Great range of mature plants

Tendercare
Southlands Road, Denham
Middlesex, UK9 4HD
Tel: 01895 835544
www.tendercare.co.uk
Mature hardy plants

Thompson Landscapes.com
Tel: 01923 260 190
www.thompsonlandscapes.com
*Construction and installation of
water features, paving, planting*

Bamber Wallis Design
Tel: 01252 7115 139
*Design and installation of water
features*

Patio
100 Tooting Road, London
SW17 8BC. Tel: 020 8672 2251
*Range of pots, specializing in
terracotta*

Indian Ocean Trading Co
Tel: 020 8675 4808
www.indian-ocean.co.uk
Furniture

Boldstone Sculpture
Tel: 020 8568 9624
www.boldstonesculpture.co.uk
Sculpture

John Cullen Lighting
www.johncullenlighting.co.uk
Lighting effects

Garden Architecture
259 Munster Road, London
SW6 6BW. Tel: 020 7385 1020
www.gardenarchitecture.net
*Sculptures, lighting, trellis,
installation*

USA

Smith & Hawken
www.smith-hawken.com
*Furniture, containers, ornaments,
lighting*

Lazy-Man, Inc.
Tel: 908 475 5315
www.lazyman.com
Barbeques

Garden Concepts
PO Box 241233
Memphis TN 38124-1233
Tel: 901 756 1649
www.gardenconcepts.net
Furniture, trellis

The Terence Conran Shop USA
Bridgemarket, 407 East 59th St,
New York NY 10022
Tel: 212 755 9079
www.conran.com
Contemporary furniture

USA Light
Tel: 800 854 8794
www.USALight.com
Lighting

Oakes Daylilies
PO Box 268, Corryton
TN37721
www.oakesdaylilies.com
Plants

Stone Forest
Dept G, PO Box 2840,
Santa Fe, NM 87504
Tel: 505 986 8883
www.stoneforest.com
Stone fountains, spheres

The Home Depot
www.HomeDepot.com
Furniture, containers

NEW ZEALAND

Garden Bronze Co.
26 Ashfield St.
Auckland 09 444 4137
www.gardenbronze.co.nz
Stone fountains, ornaments

Brustics
Tel: 0800 278 784
www.brustics.co.nz
Natural fencing

Circa
www.cmp-ltd.co.nz
Iron furniture

AUSTRALIA

Ecoscreen
Call state distributor for stockists
Decorative lattice

**Mary Moodies' Pond, Pump and
Pot Shop**
Southern Aquatic Garden Centre
110 Boundary Road, Mortdale
Tel: 02 9153 0503
Water features and plants

Wagner Solar
Call 0800 064 790 for stockists
Lighting

Annie Wilkes
The Parterre Garden
Woolahara NSW
Design, ornaments, plants

Haddonstone Pty Ltd
104-112 Bourke St
East Sydney NSW
Tel: 02 9358 6688
Stone paving and ornaments

index

Page numbers in bold refer to picture captions.

This book is dedicated to
Terence Riley

This edition is published by
Aquamarine

Aquamarine is an imprint of Anness
Publishing Ltd
Hermes House, 88-89 Blackfriars Road,
London SE1 8HA
tel. 020 7401 2077; fax 020 7633 9499
www.aquamarinebooks.com;
info@anness.com

UK agent: The Manning Partnership
Ltd; tel. 01225 478 444; fax 01225 478
440; sales@manning-partnership.co.uk

UK distributor: Grantham Book
Services Ltd; tel. 01476 541080; fax
01476 541061; orders@gbs.tbs-ltd.co.uk

This edition distributed in the USA and
Canada by National Book Network,
4501 Forbes Boulevard, Suite 200,
Lanham, MD 20706; tel. 301 459 3366;
fax 301 429 5746; www.nbnbooks.com

This edition distributed in Australia by
Pan Macmillan Australia, Level 18,
St Martins Tower, 31 Market St,
Sydney, NSW 2000; tel. 1300 135 113;
fax 1300 135 103;
customer.service@macmillan.com.au

Publisher: **Joanna Lorenz**
Managing Editor: **Helen Sudell**
Executive Editor: **Caroline Davidson**
Designer: **Elizabeth Healey**
Production Controller: **Lee Sargent**
Editorial Reader: **Penelope Goodare**
Stylist: **Jackie Hobbs**
Illustrator: **Jane Hudson**

1 2 3 4 5 6 7 8 9 10

Note to reader

The plants in this book have been given a hardiness rating (for European
readers) and a zone range (for readers in the United States):-

Hardiness Ratings

Frost tender: Plant may be damaged by temperatures below 5°C (41°F)
Half hardy: Plant can withstand temperatures down to 0°C (32°F)
Frost hardy: Plant can withstand temperatures down to −5°C (23°F)
Fully hardy: Plant can withstand temperatures down to −15°C (5°F)

Plant Hardiness Zones

The Agricultural Research Service of the U.S. Department of Agriculture has
developed a system of plant hardiness zones. Plants in the Plant Directory have
been given a zone range. The zones 1–10 are based on the average annual
minimum temperature. In the zone range, the smaller number indicates the
northernmost zone in which a plant can survive the winter and the higher number
gives the most southerly area in which it will perform consistently. Bear in mind
that factors such as altitude, wind exposure, proximity to water, soil type, snow,
night temperature, shade and the level of water received by a plant may alter a
plant's hardiness by as much as two zones.

Zone 1: Below −45°C (−50°F)
Zone 2: −45 to −40°C (−50 to −40°F)
Zone 3: −40 to −34°C (−40 to −30°F)
Zone 4: −34 to −29°C (−30 to −20°F)
Zone 5: −29 to −23°C (−20 to −10°F)

Zone 6: −23 to −18°C (−10 to 0°F)
Zone 7: −18 to −12°C (0 to 10*F)
Zone 8: −12 to −7°C (10 to 20°F)
Zone 9: −7 to −1C (20 to 30F)
Zone 10: −1C to 4C (30 to 40F)

Acknowledgements

The author would like to thank everyone
for opening their doors so generously, and
most particularly the following for their
invaluable help: Jennifer Bartlett, Rob
Cassy, Colin Cheney, Henrietta Courtauld,
Iris Kaplow, Rebecca Loncraine, Susan
Lowry, Phebe Moore, Louise and Donal
Mulryan, Albert Sanders and Margot
Wellington, Barbara Schwartz, Helen
Sudell, Anthony Thompson and his team,
and Halsted Welles and his team.

The publisher would like to thank the
following garden owners, designers and
institutions for kindly allowing their gardens
to be photographed for the purposes of
this book. All photographs were taken by
Steven Wooster, unless otherwise stated.

t = top b = bottom m = middle
l = left r = right

Julie Ackers, London roof terrace: p71br,
p99l, p142. **An Auckland Garden**, designer
Rod Barnett & David Mitchell, metal
sculpture by Marte Szirmay, New Zealand:
p54, p75b. **J Bartlett** (owner and designer),
with Madison Cox (designer), New York:
p21, p32t, p42br, p94, p97t. **Marjorie
Carson**, Christchurch, New Zealand: p45t.
Colefax Building, London, designer
Michèle Osborne: p47t, p63b, p68, p83b,
p141br. **Covent Garden**, London, designer
Maria Ornberg: p11t, p74, p77bl, p81l.
Docklands roof terrace, London, garden
designer Andy Sturgeon, garden built by
The Garden Builders, sculpture supplied by
Garden Architecture: p28, p29m, p82b, p83t,
p90. **The Earth Pledge Green Roof
Initiative**, New York: p93br, p104t, p104bl,
p105. **Eric Ellis** (designer), New Zealand,
planting by Tom Gunn: p43b, p70b. **Andy
Goodsir**, Liverpool Grove, London,
designer Michèle Osborne: p23t, p31, p41b,
p69bl. **Iris Kaplow** (designer), New York:
p69t, p75t, p141tl. **London roof terrace**,
designer Luciano Giubbillei: p19b, p23b,
p41t, p72l, p76, p95b. **London Roof Terrace**,
designer Martin Summers: p135tr. **Dougald
Mabin**, Liverpool Grove, London, designer
Michèle Osborne: p29t, p46b. **Trevyn
McDowell**, 8, p46t, p96b (designer Paul
Thompson). **Millennium Harbour**, London,
designer Michèle Osborne: p5, p12t, p30r,
p60, p65tr, p86-89 (all), p136l, endpapers.
New York roof garden: p15, p25t, p52,
p104br. **New York roof garden**, designer
Halsted Welles: p1, p2, p34-7 (all), p50,
p55t, p69br, p78b, p79tl/tlm, p93bl, p134t,
p138/9t. **New York roof garden**, designer
Halsted Welles: p4, p8, p13b, p24, p45bl,
p49t, p51, p64t, p71t, p95t, p96t, p100, p101,
p102l, p102br, p103tl, p134b. **New York roof
garden**, designer Halsted Welles: p16, p33t,
p64b, p97bl, p135b, p138b. **New York roof
garden**, designer Halsted Welles: p20, p48,
p92, p106b, p114bl, p135tl. **New York roof
garden**, designer Halsted Welles, planting
by John Carloftis: p12b, p44b, p62, p67t,
p97br, p99tl/tr, p103r, p108-111 (all), p129br,
p137tl. **Michèle Osborne**, Liverpool Grove,
London (owner and designer): p6, p13t,
p42l, p56-59 (all), p79bl, p80br, p97bml/bmr,
p136b. **Paul Singleton and Andy Male**,
Liverpool Grove, London (owners and
designers): p29b, p49bm, p69m, p70t,
p77bm/br, p82t, p144. **Ted Smyth**, (designer)
New Zealand: p43t, p67br.
Soanes garden, London, designer
Henrietta Courtauld: p42tr, p73t, p98.
Martin Summers, (owner and designer),
London: 25b, p33bl/br, p44t, p45br, p53t,
p73ml/mr, p77t, p138t, p139b. **Sumner
Garden**, New Zealand, designer Erik Ellis:
p10 (both), p75b, p137b. **Richard Watson
and Nadene Ghouri**, Liverpool Grove,
London, designer Michèle Osborne: p30l,
p63t, p78t, p80br. **Tish York-Mitchell**, Old
Mutual Securities Roof Garden, London,
designer Maria Ornberg: p67m, p72r, p93t,
p102tr.
Chelsea Flower Show 2002
'A Forgotten Future', designer Michelle
Brown; p66tl, p103bl. 'The Accenture
Garden: Through the Glass Ceiling',
designer Miriam Book; p80l. 'Elevation',
designers Eric de Maeijer & Jane Hudson;
p32b, p67bl, p80tr. 'Great North Garden',
designer Alan Capper; p66b. 'Reflections in
a Tateshina Meadow', designer Miss Kay
Yamada; p65br. 'Wherefore Art Thou?',
designers Sarah Brodie & Faith Dewhurst:
p53b.

The Publishers would also like to thank the
following photographers and picture
agencies for allowing their images to be
reproduced in this book.
The Garden Picture Library: p9 (photo by
John Ferro Sims); p19t (photo by Ron
Sutherland); p22b (designer Duane Paul
Design Team); p85b (photo by Andrea
Jones); p107t (photo Ron Sutherland,
designer John Zerming); p128bl; p131bl.
John Glover: p66tr (designer Dan Pearson);
p84 (designer Stephen Crisp); p106t; p107b.
Clive Nichols: p14, p40 (both designs by
Stephen Woodhams); p79r (designer Nin
Thalinson of Lust & Fagring, Lustgard,
Sweden); p80mr (designer Trevyn
McDowell).
Photos Horticultural/Capel Manor: p81r,
designer Hilary Neiland.
Jo Whitworth: p49bl/br (designer Carolynn
Blythe).
Steven Wooster: p18 (designer Michèle
Osborne); p22t (designer Luciano
Giubbilei); p26t, p26b (designer Marshall
Cook); p27 'Courtyard Garden' Chelsea
Flower Show, (design by Brinsbury
College); p55b (designer Michèle
Osborne); p71bl RIBA Café, London, p73b
(designer Nigel Cameron); p137tr 'A
Movable Modular Garden', Chelsea Flower
Show 2001 (designer Natalie Charles).

The Publishers would also like to thank the
following companies for kindly lending items
for the purposes of photography: The Kew
Gardener, 0208 948 1422 for plants and
shrubs; The Pier, 0207 436 9642 and The
Lemon Tree 0208 546 5197 for accessories,
Katherine Gilmour 0208 673 2745 for antique
textiles, and The Indian Ocean Trading
Company www.indian-ocean.co.uk for
furniture.